GROSS FACTopia!

Follow the TRAIL of 400 ~~Foul~~ FACTS

BY PAIGE TOWLER

Illustrated by ANDY SMITH

BRITANNICA BOOKS

CONTENTS

WELCOME BACK TO FACTOPIA!

But be warned: Things are about to get... foul.

It's time to set off on an adventure through hundreds of the ickiest, stickiest, creepiest, crawliest, disgustingly marvelous, and mind-blowing facts. For example...

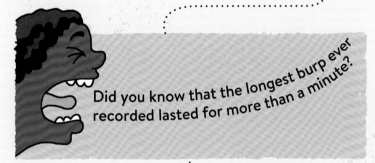

Did you know that the longest burp ever recorded lasted for more than a minute?

Read about revolting world records! One man holds a record for squirting milk from his eye.

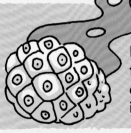

Dig into facts about foul foods like the *Morinda citrifolia*, which smells so bad it's known as the "vomit fruit."

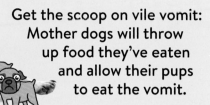

Get the scoop on vile vomit: Mother dogs will throw up food they've eaten and allow their pups to eat the vomit.

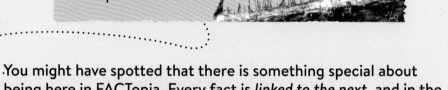

And speaking of baby animals, did you know that baby vampire aphids drink their parents' blood?

You might have spotted that there is something special about being here in FACTopia. Every fact is *linked to the next*, and in the most surprising and even hilarious ways.

On this slimiest of FACTopia tours, you will encounter **terrible toilets**, **repulsive world records**, **vile vomit**, **horrible history**, and... well, you'll see. Discover what each turn of the page will bring!

But there isn't just one trail through this book. Your path branches every now and then, and you can **wriggle backward** or **hurl forward** to a totally different (*but still connected*) part of FACTopia.

Let your curiosity take you wherever it leads. Of course, a good place to start could be right here, at the beginning..................

For example, slither your way through

this detour to find out about scaly snakes

Go to page 162

During the

GREAT STINK

of 1858, the River Thames in London was clogged with human waste. It smelled so bad that many people left the city—even the government considered moving....

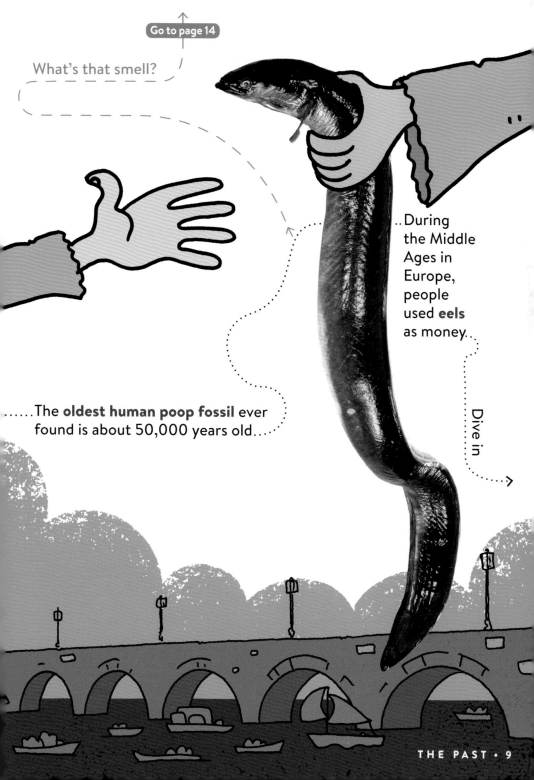

Go to page 14

What's that smell?

..During the Middle Ages in Europe, people used **eels** as money..

......The **oldest human poop fossil** ever found is about 50,000 years old....

Dive in

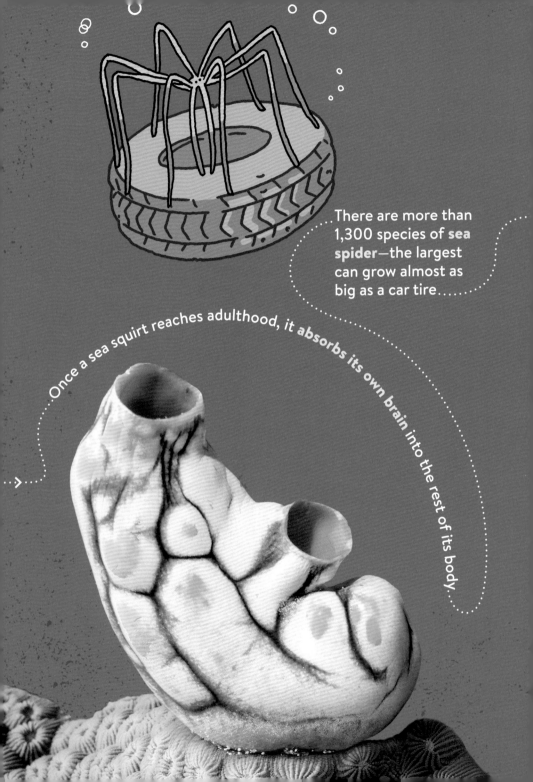

There are more than 1,300 species of **sea spider**—the largest can grow almost as big as a car tire......

Once a sea squirt reaches adulthood, it absorbs its own brain into the rest of its body.

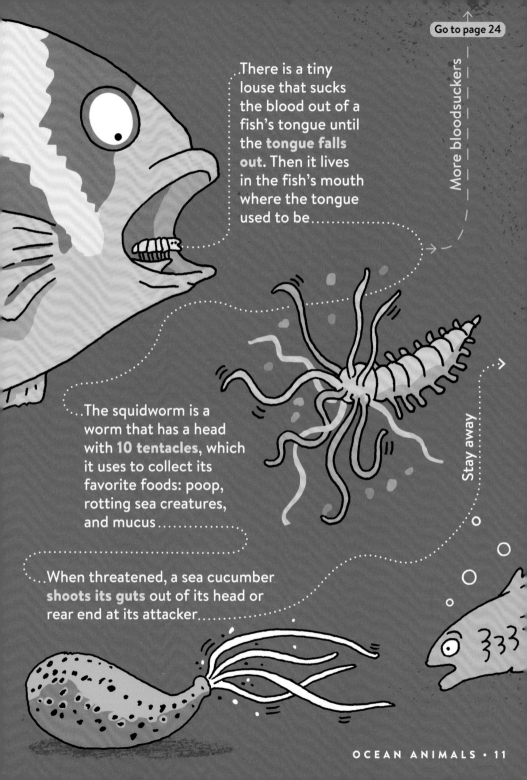

There is a tiny louse that sucks the blood out of a fish's tongue until **the tongue falls out**. Then it lives in the fish's mouth where the tongue used to be.

Go to page 24

More bloodsuckers

Stay away

The squidworm is a worm that has a head with **10 tentacles**, which it uses to collect its favorite foods: poop, rotting sea creatures, and mucus.

When threatened, a sea cucumber **shoots its guts** out of its head or rear end at its attacker.

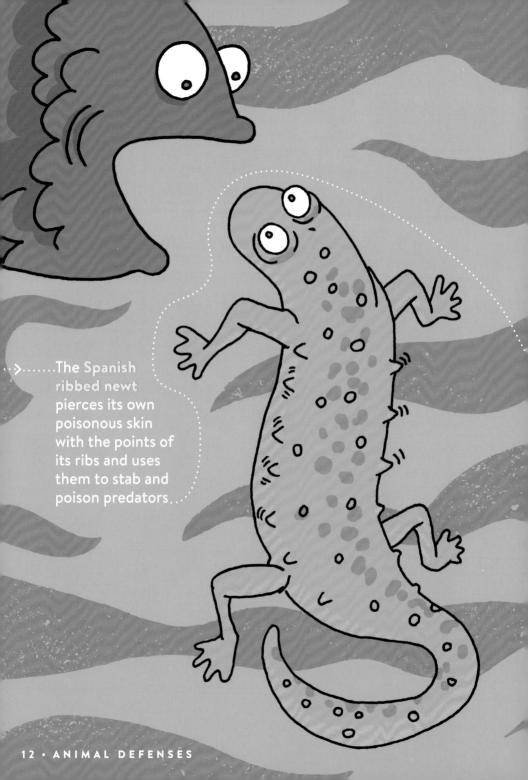

The Spanish ribbed newt pierces its own poisonous skin with the points of its ribs and uses them to stab and poison predators.

To defend itself, a spotted skunk does a **handstand** to intimidate any predators... and if that doesn't work, it sprays a foul-smelling liquid from scent glands near the base of its tail...

Pee-yew!

More toxic animals

Go to page 106

Seal Island, off the coast of Cape Town, South Africa, is said to be the **WORST-SMELLING**

PLACE ON EARTH.

It's home to up to 75,000 Cape fur seals whose poop smells like rotting fish.

Oh, poo

To lure their dung beetle prey, burrowing owls collect animal poop and bring it to their dens.

Hippopotamuses **spin their tails** while they poop. The spinning flings their dung up to 33 feet (10m), helping hippos mark their territory.

Hippos deposit nearly 40 tons (36t) of poop into the Mara River in Kenya, Africa, every day. The poop actually helps keep the river healthy.

Go to page 92

Poop explosion!

Sloths poop only **once a week**.

Call the doctor!

"Poop pills" contain healthy bacteria found in a person's poop. The pills can be given as medicine for certain infections.

Some doctors in ancient Rome and Greece prescribed a treatment for headaches that involved jolting patients with a live **electric eel**

Ancient Egyptian doctors believed that they could **cure toothaches** by placing half a dead mouse on the painful tooth.

More mice

Go to page 146

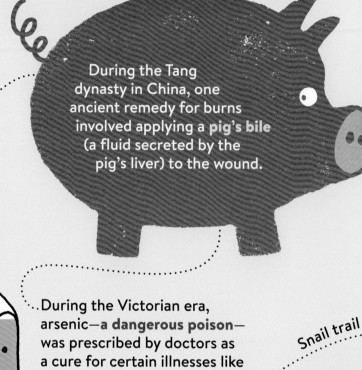

During the Tang dynasty in China, one ancient remedy for burns involved applying a **pig's bile** (a fluid secreted by the pig's liver) to the wound.

During the Victorian era, arsenic—**a dangerous poison**—was prescribed by doctors as a cure for certain illnesses like asthma and diabetes.

Snail trail ....>

Since ancient times, people around the world have been healing sore throats with **snail slime**—and some companies still make medicine using this "snail syrup" today.

Snail shells have been used as nests by bees and **wasps**.

Fossils have been preserved in guano— the poop from **bats**.

Tapeworm eggs were discovered in a 270-million-year-old shark poop **fossil**.

There are **bat-eating** spiders.

The webs of spiders have been used throughout history as **bandages**.

One type of wasp lays its eggs inside a ladybug's belly. The eggs hatch, spin themselves a cocoon, and take over the ladybug's brain—turning it into a real-life zombie.

Wasp babies in here!

Zombie worms feed on the bones of dead whales.

Whales can get tapeworms—parasitic worms that live in animal intestines—that can grow more than 16 times as long as an adult human is tall.

Don't scratch!

It could take up to 4,037 square feet (375sq m) of bandages to wrap a mummy—that's almost enough to cover a basketball court.

Mummies have been found with lice.

The **itchy feeling** from lice is actually caused by the body's reaction to the bug's saliva.

BLOOD TYPE

A+

BLOOD TYPE

B-

Lice feed on blood up to **five times a day**, and they usually prefer to dine on the same types of blood for their entire lives....

Mmm tasty!

BLOOD TYPE

0+

BLOOD TYPE

AB+

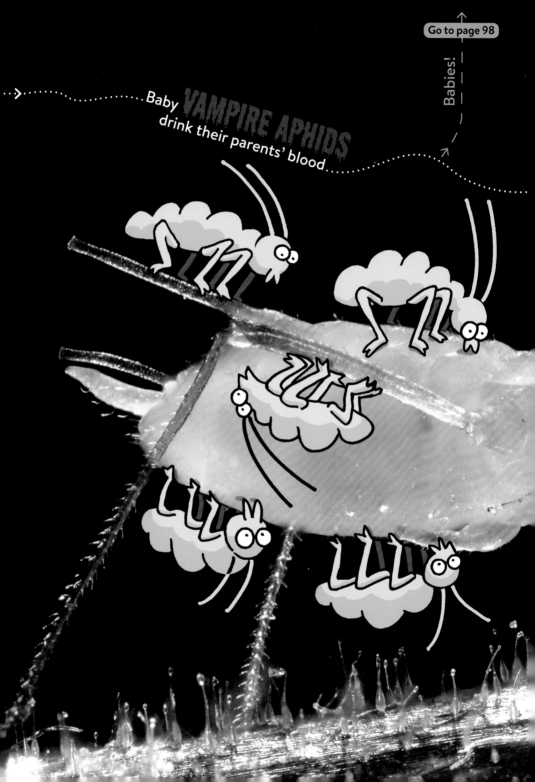

Go to page 98

Babies!

VAMPIRE APHIDS

Baby drink their parents' blood

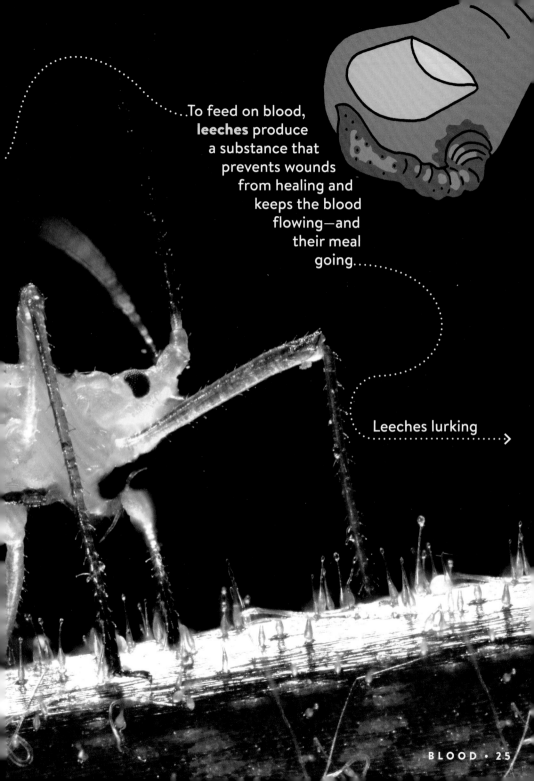

To feed on blood, **leeches** produce a substance that prevents wounds from healing and keeps the blood flowing—and their meal going.

Leeches lurking

Leeches have **34 brains**.

The largest leech in the world, the giant Amazon leech, can grow to about the length of a **house cat** (not including the cat's tail).

Here, kitty!

Some leeches have three sets of jaws and up to **300 teeth**.

Go to page 134

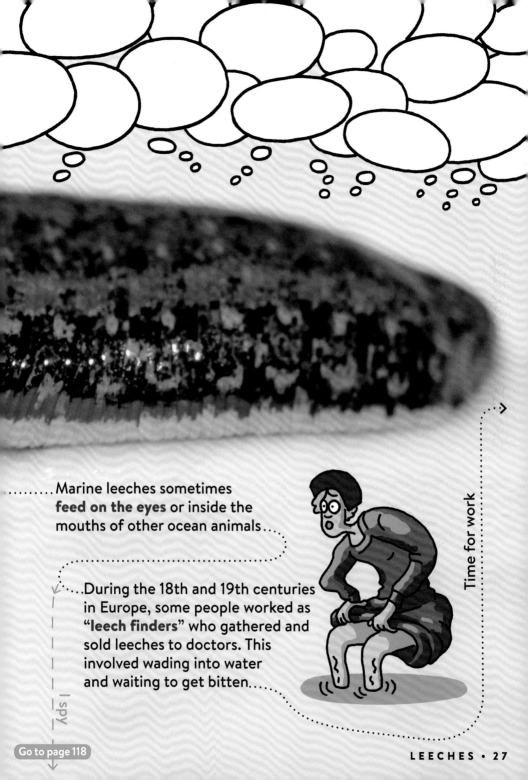

..........Marine leeches sometimes
feed on the eyes or inside the
mouths of other ocean animals...

....During the 18th and 19th centuries
in Europe, some people worked as
"**leech finders**" who gathered and
sold leeches to doctors. This
involved wading into water
and waiting to get bitten...

Time for work

I spy

Go to page 118

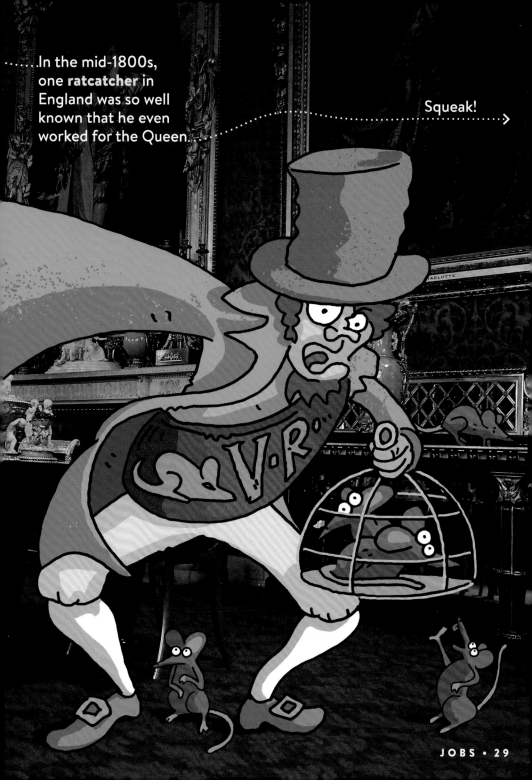

In the mid-1800s, one **ratcatcher** in England was so well known that he even worked for the Queen.

Squeak!

Go to page 90

A "**rat king**" is a tangled ball of rats whose tails are knotted together. Experts think most documented rat kings have been hoaxes, but it's possible rat kings may actually occur in very rare situations—like when rats' tails get caught in frozen clumps of their pee and poop...

Where's the toilet?

Rats breed so quickly that just one pair of rats can have up to 15,000 descendants—includin

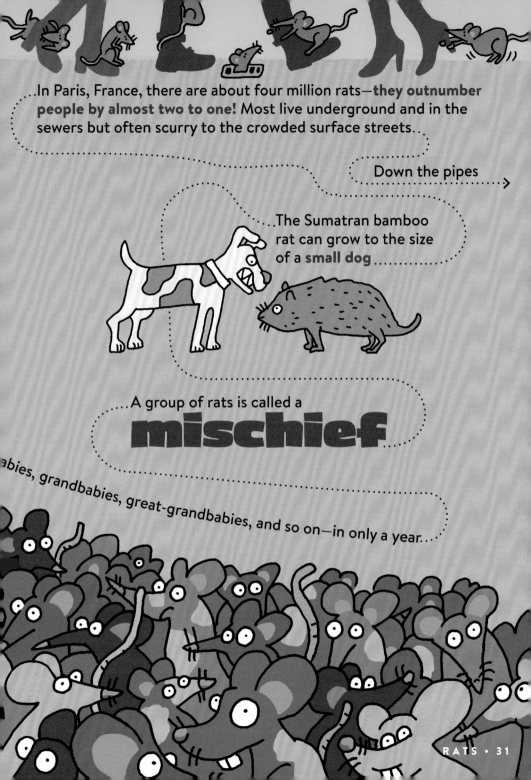

In Paris, France, there are about four million rats—**they outnumber people by almost two to one!** Most live underground and in the sewers but often scurry to the crowded surface streets.

Down the pipes ›

The Sumatran bamboo rat can grow to the size of a **small dog**.

A group of rats is called a

mischief

abies, grandbabies, great-grandbabies, and so on—in only a year.

Sewers sometimes develop massive **fatbergs**—solid chunks of fat, oil, and wet wipes that people have poured down their drains...

In the 19th century, people known as "toshers" would descend into the sewers of London to **hunt for lost coins** and valuable metals.

In Australia, pythons have been found slithering through the sewers.

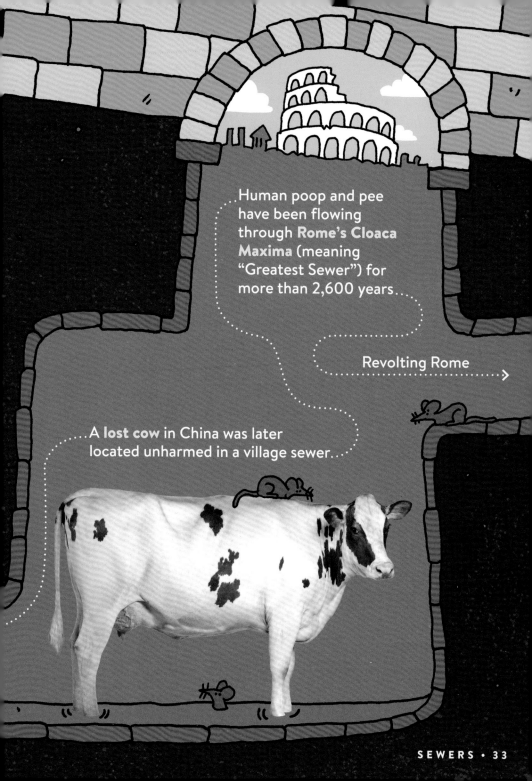

Human poop and pee have been flowing through **Rome's Cloaca Maxima** (meaning "Greatest Sewer") for more than 2,600 years.

Revolting Rome →

A **lost cow** in China was later located unharmed in a village sewer.

Ancient Romans sometimes purchased souvenir vials of gladiator sweat.

Sweat contains some of the same chemicals found in skunk spray.

The skunk ape is a legendary apelike creature that is said to smell terrible and lurk in American swamps.

A type of millipede that lived about 300 million years ago grew to about the length of an adult cheetah.

One zoo's cheetah cubs celebrated their first birthdays with ice, chunks of meat, chicken broth, and animal blood—all made into a cake!

Rotting wood, chewed leaves, and poop are the main ingredients of a North American millipede's nest.

One guest brought a 125-year-old cake onto a television show—and the host ate a bite on air.

Television remotes can carry more bacteria than a toilet seat.

Up to 50,000 different species of bacteria can be found in just one gram of soil.

People dive into **swamps** in Finland to play soccer as part of the Swamp Soccer **competitions**.

At one stinky **competition** in New York City, the winner is the kid whose shoes have the most revolting **smell**.

To make a spray that can cover up the worst of **smells**, one perfume company studied the chemicals from **toilets** in four different countries.

After using the **toilet**, people in ancient Japan and China would often use small pieces of **wood** to wipe their bottoms!

There's no making this up.

"Night **soil**" is a name for fertilizer made from human **poop**.

Poop from crocodiles was sometimes used as makeup by women in ancient Rome.

Fish scales are sometimes added to makeup

Lanolin—the oil that oozes from sheep skin—is an ingredient in many **lip balms**.

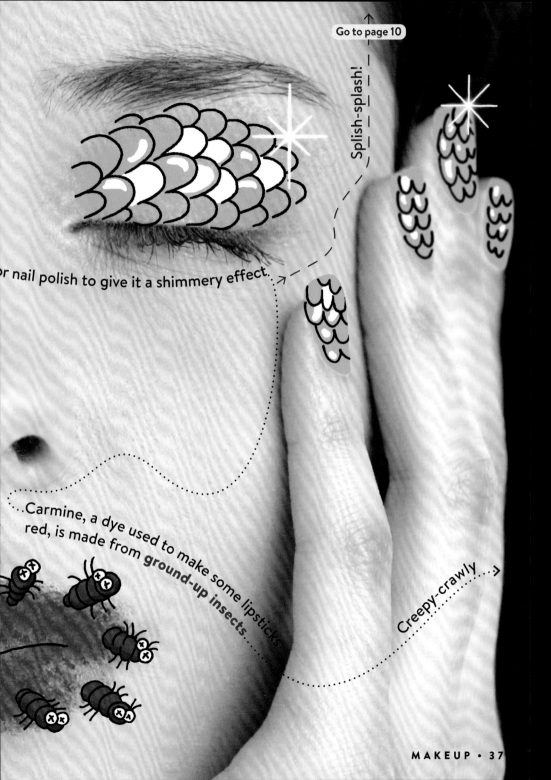

Go to page 10

Splish-splash!

or nail polish to give it a shimmery effect.

Carmine, a dye used to make some lipsticks red, is made from **ground-up insects**.

Creepy-crawly

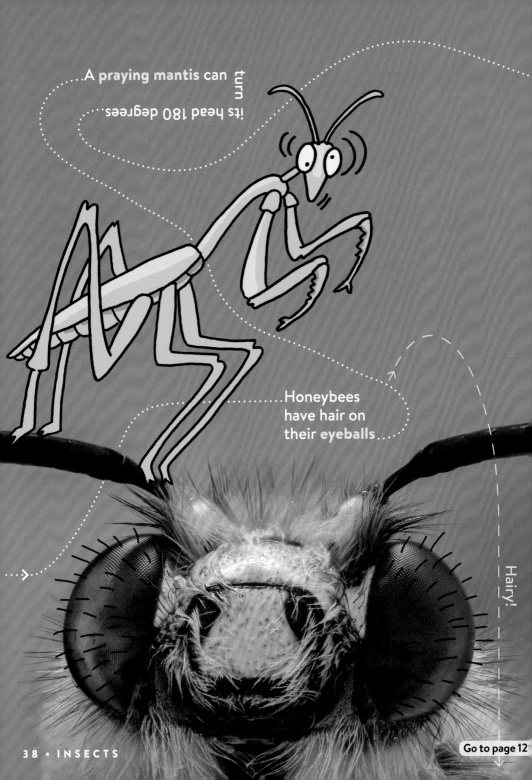

A praying mantis can turn its head 180 degrees

Honeybees have hair on their eyeballs

Hairy!

Go to page 12

The
TITAN BEETLE

can grow as big as an adult human's hand.

Yum!

...Ladybug babies often **eat their own siblings** and any unhatched eggs.

Poop from the lac bug is used to make shellac, an ingredient in **jelly beans** and other shiny candies

Eager for eggs?

Go to page 94

Go to page 52

Blow a bubble

Gumballs contain lanolin—the greasy oil found in sheep's wool.

Some companies make fizzy candy that comes in a container shaped like a toilet

Flush it!

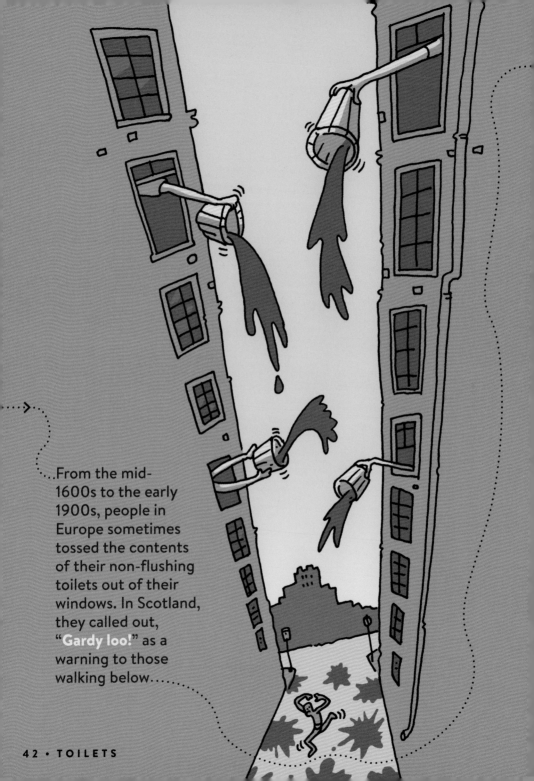

From the mid-1600s to the early 1900s, people in Europe sometimes tossed the contents of their non-flushing toilets out of their windows. In Scotland, they called out, **"Gardy loo!"** as a warning to those walking below......

In ancient Rome, a public toilet usually had **multiple seats** for several people to use at the same time......

Go back in time

Go to page 8

Scientists studying the toilets of a castle in Cyprus found that they still contained human poop that was more than 800 years old... and filled with the remains of parasites—organisms that live in or on other organisms to survive..

Invasion!

An adult bedbug is the size and shape of an **apple seed**.

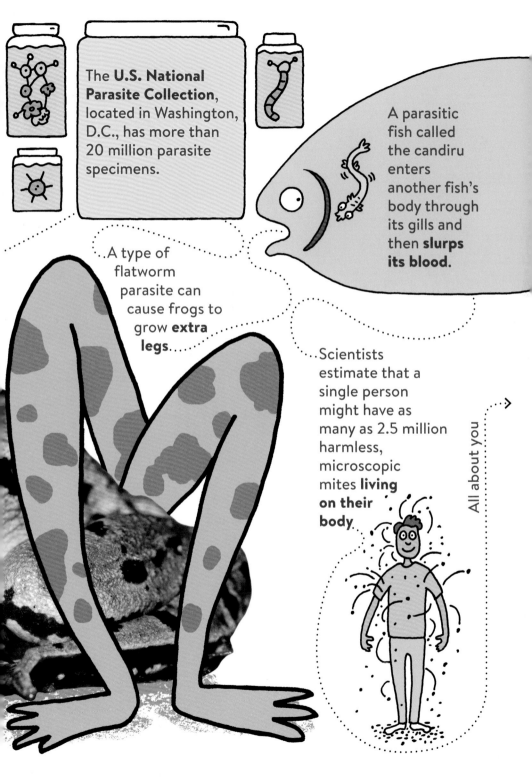

The **U.S. National Parasite Collection**, located in Washington, D.C., has more than 20 million parasite specimens.

A parasitic fish called the candiru enters another fish's body through its gills and then **slurps its blood.**

A type of flatworm parasite can cause frogs to grow **extra legs.**

Scientists estimate that a single person might have as many as 2.5 million harmless, microscopic mites **living on their body.**

All about you

In one study, scientists discovered more than 1,000 previously unknown species of bacteria living in people's **belly buttons**.

Go to page 100

I'm gonna be sick

Germy!

Stomach spasms can cause a person to **SPEW VOMIT** farther than the length of a small car.

both vomit and **Parmesan cheese**......... Say cheese!

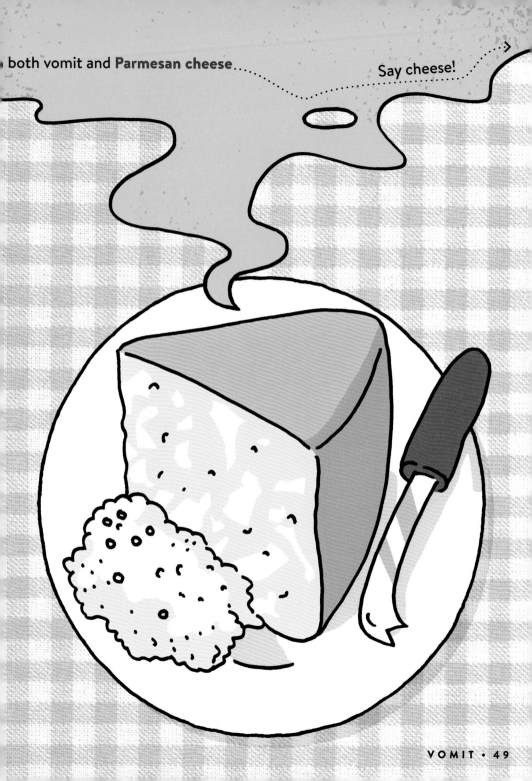

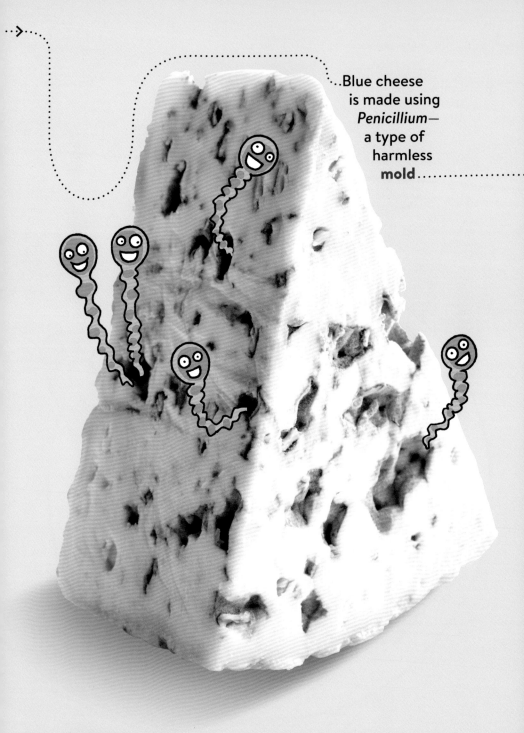

Blue cheese is made using *Penicillium*— a type of harmless **mold**

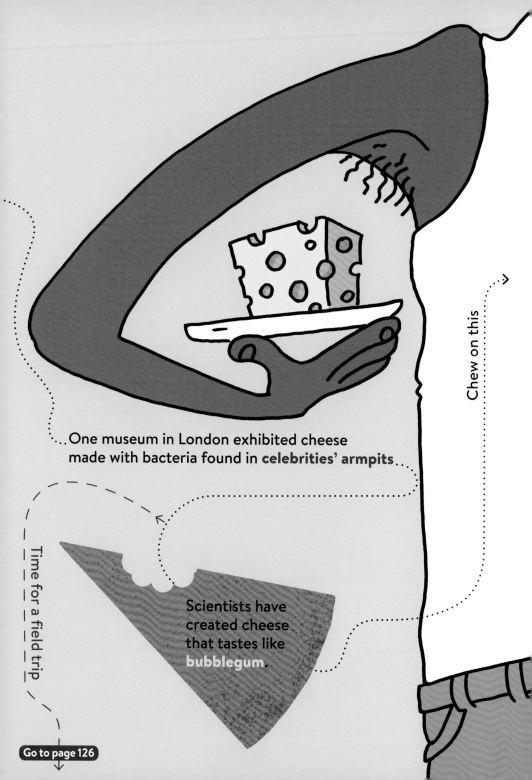

One museum in London exhibited cheese made with bacteria found in **celebrities' armpits**

Scientists have created cheese that tastes like **bubblegum**.

Chew on this

Time for a field trip

Go to page 126

A famous landmark known as the **Gum Wall** in Seattle, Washington, features hundreds of thousands of pieces of chewed-up gum that visitors have left behind.

An American woman set a world record by blowing a gum bubble larger than the diameter of a soccer ball... **with her nose.**

How artsy!

Go to page 174

Scientists are studying the saliva left on a piece of ancient gum that someone **chewed up and spat out** more than 5,700 years ago.

Ptooey!

At **cherry-spitting competitions** around the world, people compete to see who can spit a cherry pit the farthest....

....The average adult creates up to 0.4 gallons (1.5L) of saliva each day—enough to fill more than *four soda cans*....

Go to page 180

Bath time

One kind of spider catches its prey by spitting a **sticky silk** that traps the meal in place

Come into my web

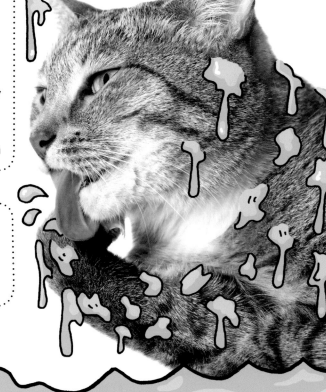

While grooming, **cats cover themselves in saliva**—and germs. One study discovered almost a million bacteria per gram of cat hair

Your spit starts **breaking down** the food you eat even before you swallow it

...Orb weaver spiders **vomit a special fluid** all over their prey that helps soften it so the spider can chew up its victim until it's liquefied. Then, it sucks up the liquid....

...The Darwin's bark spider can build a web large enough to **span a river.**

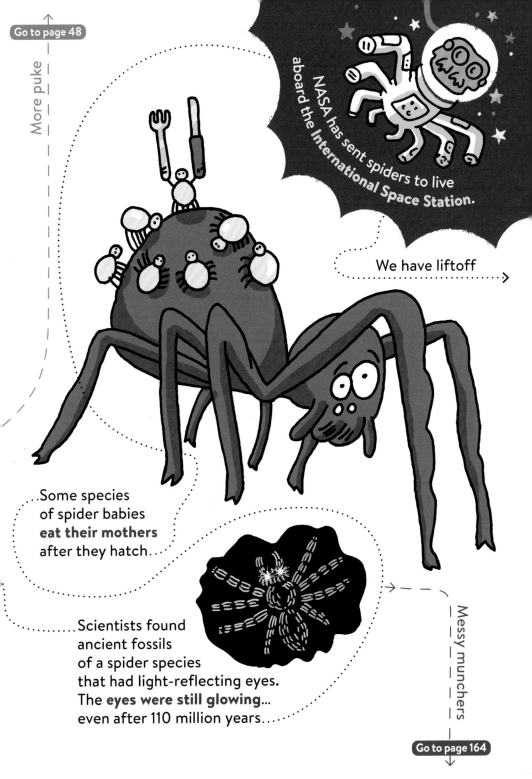

Go to page 48

More puke

NASA has sent spiders to live aboard the **International Space Station**.

We have liftoff →

Some species of spider babies **eat their mothers** after they hatch.

Scientists found ancient fossils of a spider species that had light-reflecting eyes. The **eyes were still glowing**... even after 110 million years.

Messy munchers

Go to page 164

To train future astronauts for space, NASA uses zero-gravity-simulating planes, one of which made passengers so nauseated they nicknamed it the

VOMIT COMET

Astronauts wear special diapers on space walks that let them pee in their suits.

Because gas is flammable, it can be dangerous for astronauts to fart while in space.

Let it rip!

What an outfit!

Go to page 108

To help
them float,
manatees have
special pouches
that store
their gas.
When they
want to swim
deeper,
they pass gas.

To keep **chicken poop** from getting everywhere, some farmers put specially made diapers on their chickens.

Bring on the birds

Go to page 178

One Australian farm is powered almost entirely by the waste from its **pigs and cows**.

Goats and sheep do not have upper teeth—instead, they have a **fleshy bulge** called a dental palate.

Alpacas can be trained to use **litter boxes**.

A **chicken's brain** is partially inside its neck. Because of this, one chicken survived a whole year without a head.

Feeling brainy?

Take a bite

Go to page 102

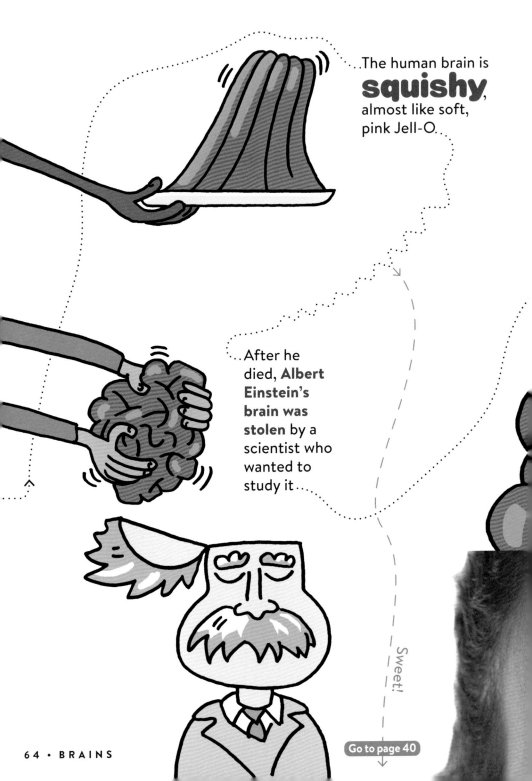

The human brain is **squishy**, almost like soft, pink Jell-O.

After he died, **Albert Einstein's brain was stolen** by a scientist who wanted to study it

Sweet!

Go to page 40

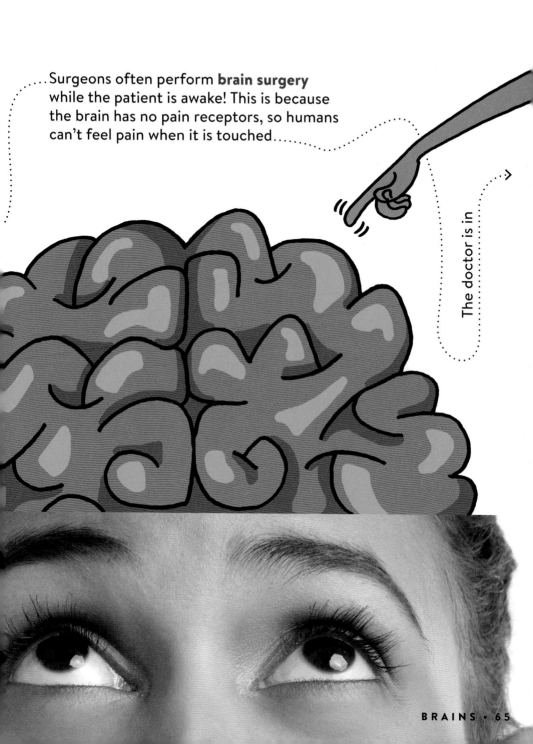

Surgeons often perform **brain surgery** while the patient is awake! This is because the brain has no pain receptors, so humans can't feel pain when it is touched......

The doctor is in

As early as 10,000 BCE, humans were practicing a type of surgery called trepanation. This involved drilling a hole into the patient's skull

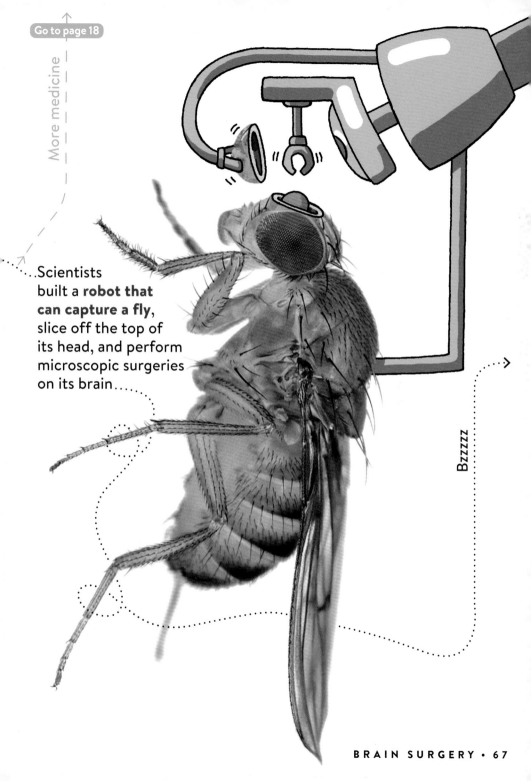

Go to page 18

More medicine

Scientists built a **robot that can capture a fly**, slice off the top of its head, and perform microscopic surgeries on its brain.

Bzzzzz

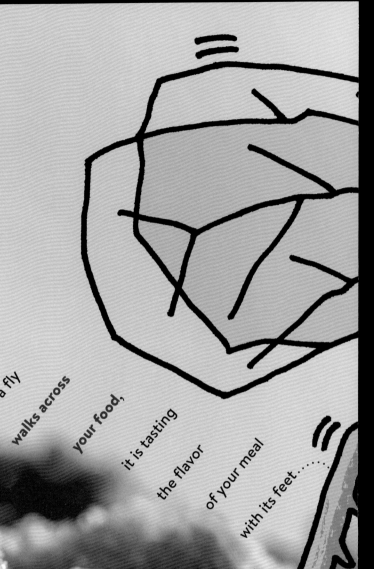

When a fly walks across your food, it is tasting the flavor of your meal with its feet....

Funky feet

In order to heal wounds, animal **poop** was sometimes applied directly to a cut by **ancient Roman** doctors.

Nightingale **bird poop** is the main ingredient in a popular face cream!

One **ancient Roman** writer believed that a person could tell the future by swallowing a **mole**'s heart while it was still beating.

Vomit makes up most of the diet of the skua **bird**.

The **smell** of a fruit called the *Morinda citrifolia* earned it the nickname "**vomit** fruit."

The foot, or the bottom of a **slug**, is covered in mucus.

Slug soup was used by **doctors** as an antidote for certain poisons in the Middle Ages.

Since ancient Roman times, some people in Europe have believed that wearing a **mole**'s **mummified** paws or teeth could ward off cramps and toothaches.

An almost perfectly preserved **mummified** wolf—missing only its eyes but still covered in fur and leathery skin—was created 57,000 years ago when it was suddenly buried in **mud**.

People run through a **mud**-soaked obstacle course for 10 miles (16km) as part of the Tough Mudder competition.

Dinosaurs may have been attracted to the rotting **smell** of ginkgo tree berries.

Colonies of **bacteria** can live inside **dinosaur** bones—even after they've been fossilized.

Go for gold!

Medieval **doctors** often tried to diagnose illnesses by sniffing or tasting their patients' **pee**.

It is against the law to **pee** in the **ocean** in some parts of Spain.

Some **ocean bacteria** eat oil.

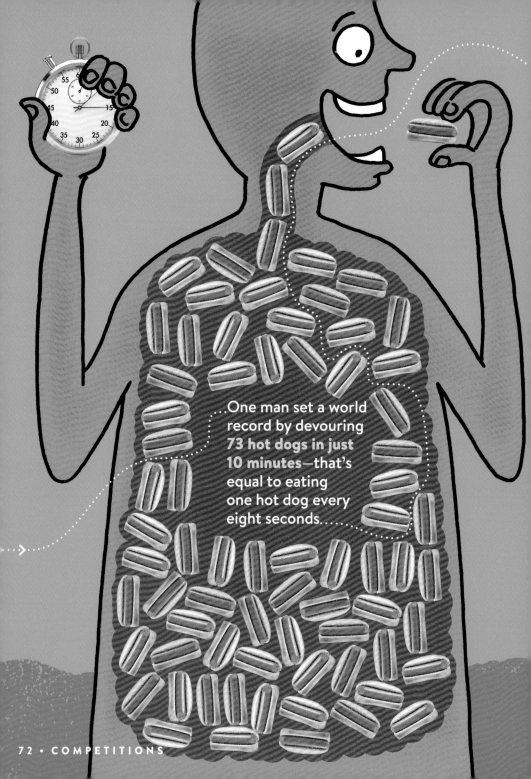

One man set a world record by devouring **73 hot dogs** in just **10 minutes**—that's equal to eating one hot dog every eight seconds.

Go to page 110

A new record

At the World Cow Chip Throwing Contest, contestants try to **toss dry cow poop the farthest.**

A television show held a contest to see who could **eat the most sticks of butter.**

During **pudding eating contests,** competitors aren't allowed to use their hands.

To educate people about insects, some schools and museums hold **cockroach races**

Ready for roaches?

Go to page 142

Shall we eat?

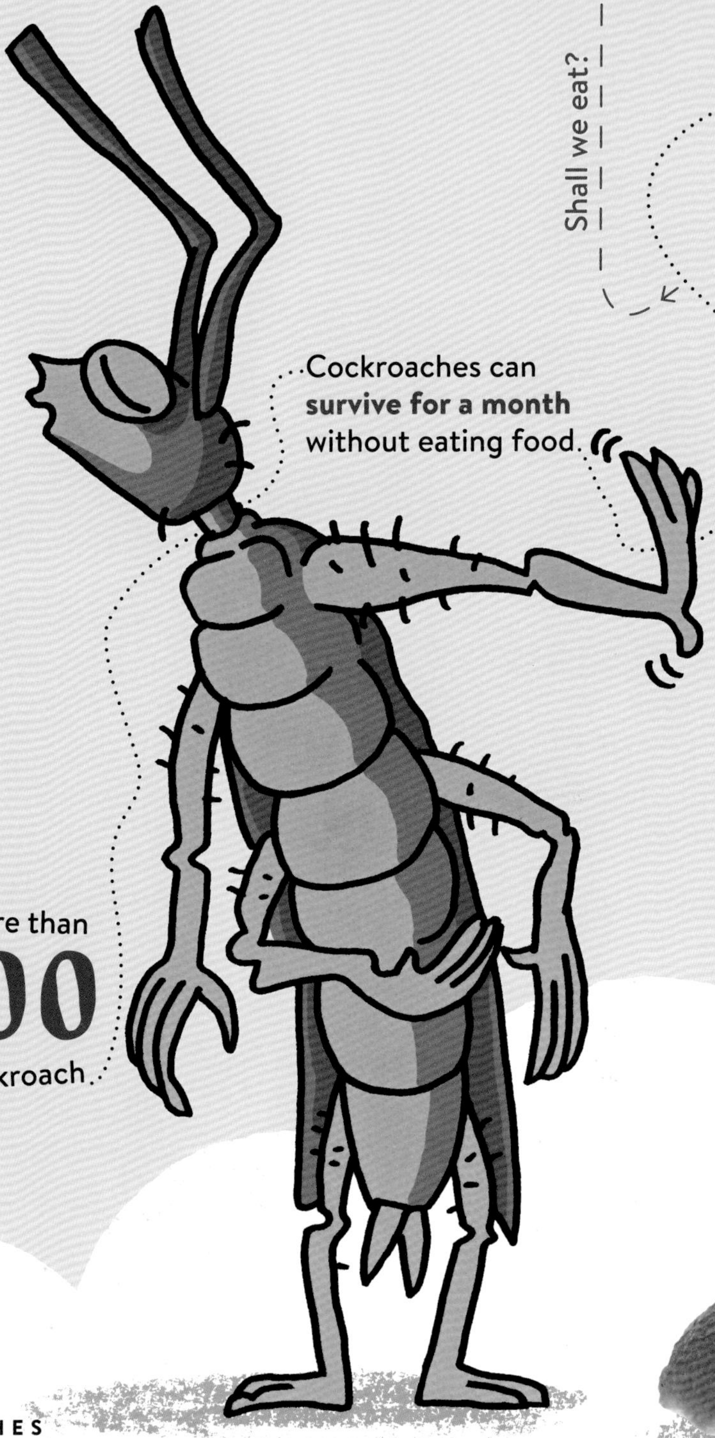

Cockroaches can **survive for a month** without eating food.

........> There are more than

4,000

species of cockroach.

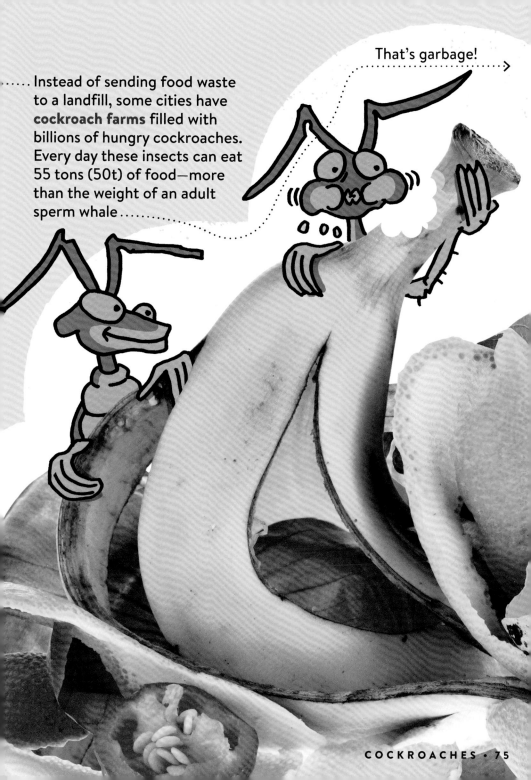

Instead of sending food waste to a landfill, some cities have **cockroach farms** filled with billions of hungry cockroaches. Every day these insects can eat 55 tons (50t) of food—more than the weight of an adult sperm whale...........

That's garbage!

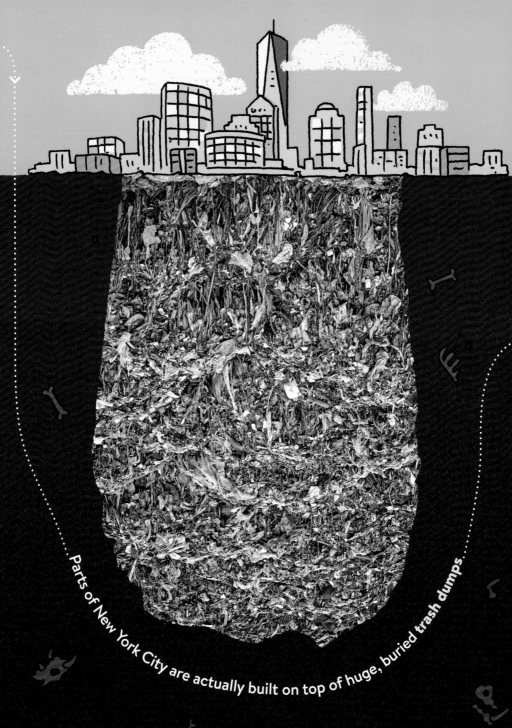

Parts of New York City are actually built on top of huge, buried trash dumps.

Go to page 32

Go underground

Make a splash!

Scientists have discovered microbes that could possibly help get rid of *plastic trash in the ocean*—by eating it

When they eat, sea stars **push their stomachs** out through their mouths to cover their meal and digest it

Other organs

Go to page 150

Thousands of microbes—including bacteria that consume iron—swarm **sunken shipwrecks** in the deep sea.

Moving deeper

To escape predators, one type of deep-sea shrimp pukes glowing **vomit**.

A "**vomit** machine" that pukes on command was created by **scientists**.

Scientists are trying to find a way to make poop **glow in the dark**. They hope it will help identify illnesses.

A **shrimp** ancestor known as *Anomalocaris* ("strange shrimp") lived more than 500 million years ago and could grow as big as a large **dog**.

Some **dogs** can be trained to ring a bell when they have to pee or **poop**.

Poop can contain foods that are too difficult for people to digest—like the shells of **corn** kernels, which are made of a material that's tough to break down.

Earthworms have five **hearts**.

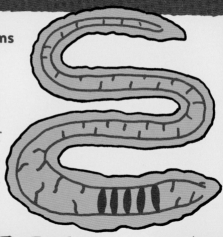

There are **glow-in-the-dark worms**.

You can see the beating **heart** of the translucent ghost **shrimp**.

All that oozing blood in old monster movies is fake; it was often made of **corn** syrup and food coloring.

Real monsters

...The **ghost octopus** has very few muscles, which gives it a goo-like, squishy texture......

Go to page 12

When Mormon crickets swarm in groups, they will often **devour one another**—especially any cricket that attempts to fly in the wrong direction.

Daring defenses

More plants

The **vampire squid** can turn itself "inside out" to avoid predators by curling its spiky bottom half over its body.

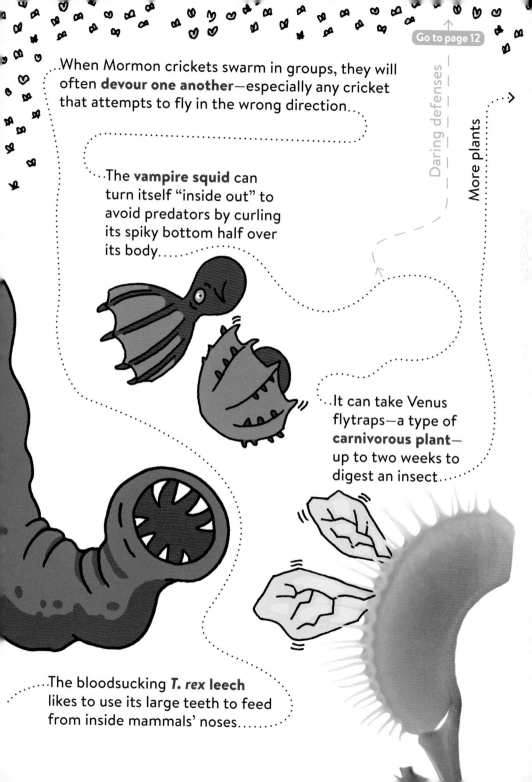

It can take Venus flytraps—a type of **carnivorous plant**—up to two weeks to digest an insect.

The bloodsucking *T. rex leech* likes to use its large teeth to feed from inside mammals' noses.

The **skunk cabbage** attracts insects with its scent; it is said to smell like skunk spray and rotting meat.

A plant called the octopus stinkhorn emits a **stench that attracts flies,** which then feast on the slime that covers the plant

What a stench!

Artificial intelligence may soon be able to re-create some historical stenches that no longer exist—such as stinky canals or dung—with the help of **scientists**.

Scientists discovered a 4,000-year-old "super colony" of termites in Brazil that covers an area roughly the length and **width** of Great Britain.

Poop-rolling dung beetles can sometimes be found "**dancing**" on top of their ball of dung.

There is a **robot** designed to pick up dog **poop**.

A kind of **dancing** spider nicknamed Skeletorus resembles a skeleton, thanks to its black-and-white stripes that look like **bones**.

Bones make up most of a bearded vulture's diet. These birds eat only the rotting bodies of animals—called **carrion**.

Carrion beetles are often covered in **mites**.

About twice the **width** of the U.S.A., the Great Atlantic Sargassum Belt in the Atlantic Ocean is the largest known **algae** bloom ever discovered.

Invasive **algae** found in rivers are known as "rock **snot**."

To research how **germs** spread, scientists built a coughing **robot**.

Snot often turns green when you are sick because your body produces more white blood cells and greenish colored iron to fight off invading **germs**.

Dust is usually made up of dirt, fiber, and human **skin**.

Human **skin** has been used to bind **books**.

Books on manners—including ones telling people not to pass gas, pick their noses, or scratch flea bites during dinner—were popular starting in the late Middle Ages.

Some kinds of **mites** live in **dust**.

Travel back in time

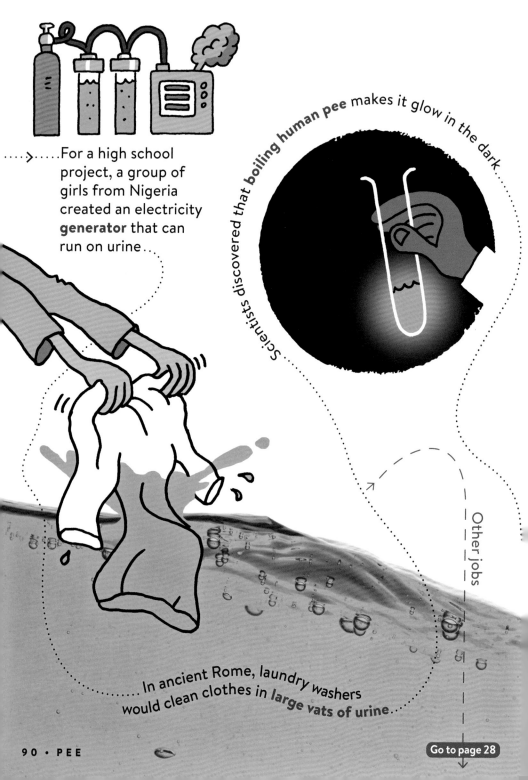

For a high school project, a group of girls from Nigeria created an electricity **generator** that can run on urine..

Scientists discovered that **boiling human pee** makes it glow in the dark..

Other jobs

In ancient Rome, laundry washers would clean clothes in large vats of urine..

Go to page 28

Go to page 122

Disgusting dinos

Pee was once used to make **gunpowder**

Boom!

According to scientists, all the fresh water on Earth has been drunk—and peed out—by **dinosaurs**.

A foam that sometimes forms on large amounts of **pig poop** can spontaneously **EXPLODE**.

When whales die, their bodies usually sink. But if the body of a dead whale washes up on shore, **gases build up inside** and can make it **EXPLODE**.

Go to page 60

This way for more gas

Rotten eggs sometimes **EXPLODE**.

Egg-cellent! →

Go to page 132

Infested!

Double-banded courser eggs resemble **antelope poop.** The bird usually lays a single egg near a poop pile to hide it from predators

In just 25 days, an African driver **ant queen** can lay three to four million eggs

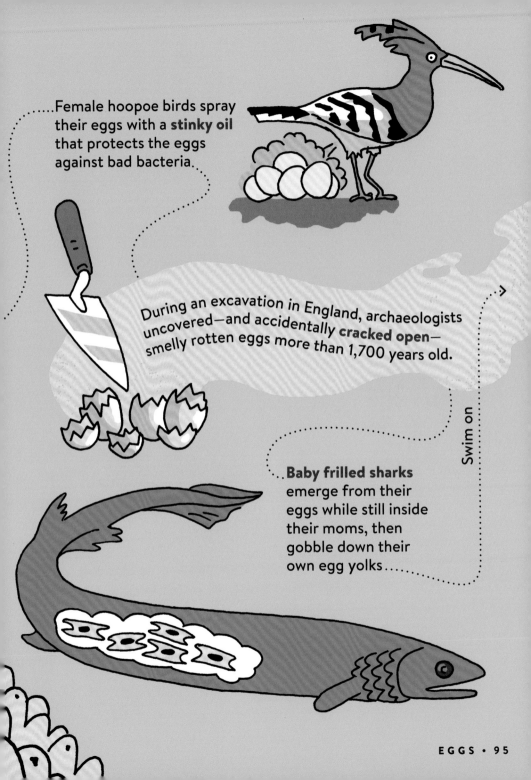

Female hoopoe birds spray their eggs with a **stinky oil** that protects the eggs against bad bacteria.

During an excavation in England, archaeologists uncovered—and accidentally **cracked open**—smelly rotten eggs more than 1,700 years old.

Baby frilled sharks emerge from their eggs while still inside their moms, then gobble down their own egg yolks

Swim on

When sharks poop,
smaller fish often
feed on the waste.

Shark poop is green.

Time to babysit!

Before they are born, baby sharks often hunt and eat each other inside their mother's womb.

Koala babies eat a liquid form of their mom's poop known as pap

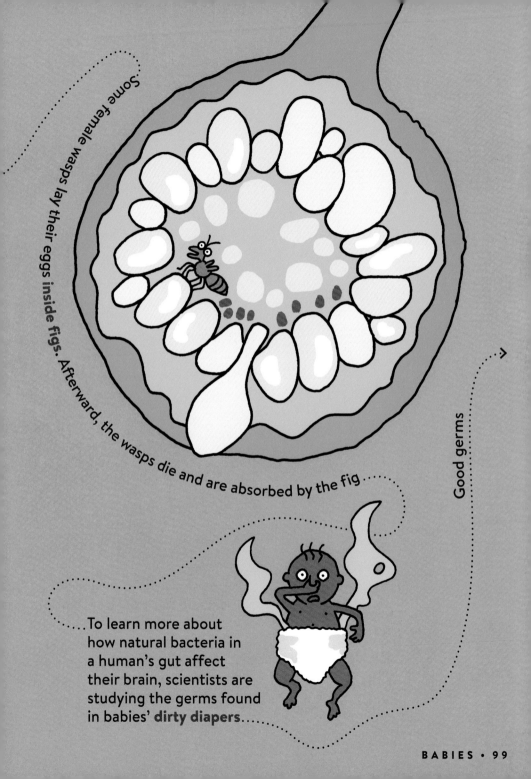

Some female wasps lay their eggs inside figs. Afterward, the wasps die and are absorbed by the fig.

Good germs

To learn more about how natural bacteria in a human's gut affect their brain, scientists are studying the germs found in babies' **dirty diapers.**

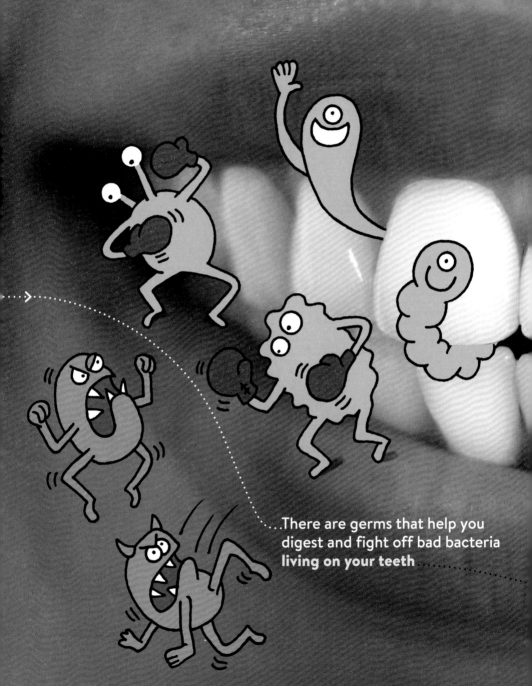

There are germs that help you digest and fight off bad bacteria living on your teeth

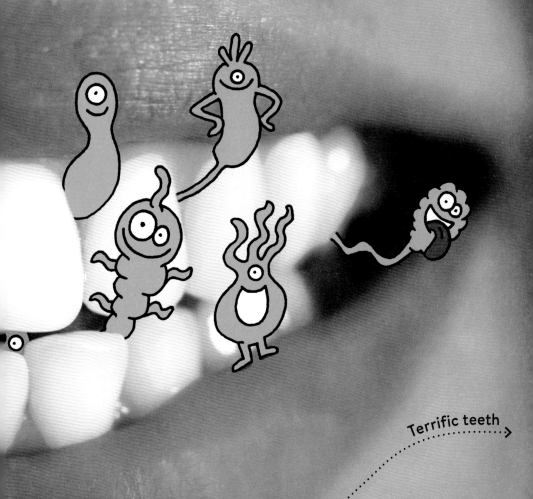

Terrific teeth ⋯⋯⋯>

Snails have thousands of teeth

One Irish legend says you can cure a toothache by putting **a frog in your mouth** (and then taking it out unharmed after you've licked it)

Hop along

Scientists think the prehistoric "**devil frog**," which weighed more than seven basketballs, may have feasted on baby dinosaurs.

In order to grow, many frogs **shed their outer layer of skin**... and then eat it.

Some species of frogs live in **elephant dung**...

The Surinam toad gives birth to her babies through **skin sacs** on her back.

Cane toads sometimes **eat each other**—even though they are poisonous to other animals.

From the rear

Something tastes funny

Go to page 116

Go to page 176

That's the pits

Slow lorises lick glands located near their armpits that coat their sharp teeth with venom.

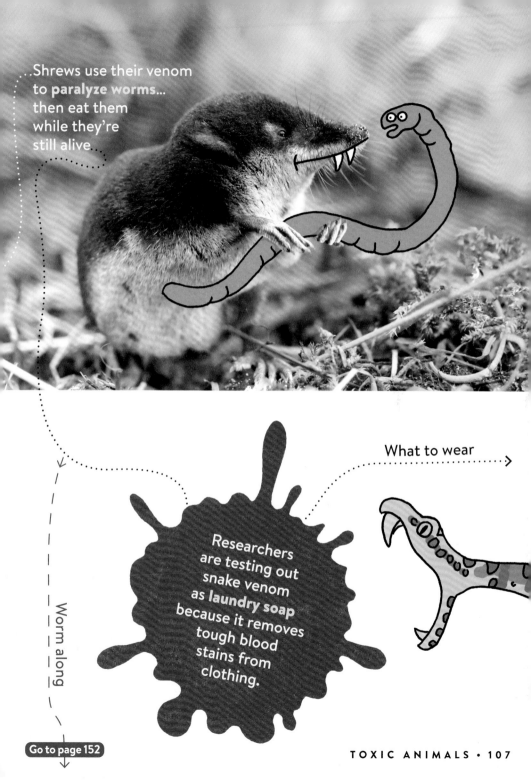

Shrews use their venom to **paralyze worms...** then eat them while they're still alive...

Worm along

Go to page 152

What to wear →

Researchers are testing out snake venom as **laundry soap** because it removes tough blood stains from clothing.

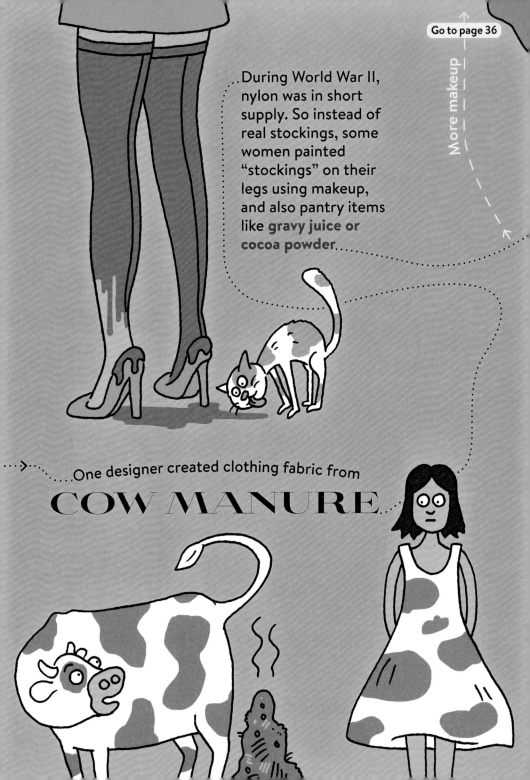

Go to page 36

More makeup

During World War II, nylon was in short supply. So instead of real stockings, some women painted "stockings" on their legs using makeup, and also pantry items like **gravy juice or cocoa powder**.

One designer created clothing fabric from

COW MANURE

The world record for the most people **changing diapers** at the same time is 8,251.

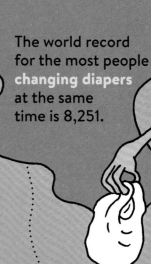

Pop star Lady Gaga once wore a dress, hat, and shoes made of

raw meat

while attending an awards show.

More record-breakers

Designers have created a type of "leather" made from **mushroom roots**

A man from the United Kingdom once set a world record by using his toes to crush **60 eggs** in one minute.

An American man set a world record by launching a marshmallow out of his nostril and into the mouth of a woman more than 17 feet (5m) away.

A man from Turkey holds a record for **squirting milk** from his eye.

Go to page 196

Follow your nose

Step this way

One man from London set a world record for moving more than 37 pounds (17kg) of **maggots** using only his mouth.

A woman from Ohio holds a world record for **foot-sniffing.** She sniffed about 5,600 feet while testing foot products.

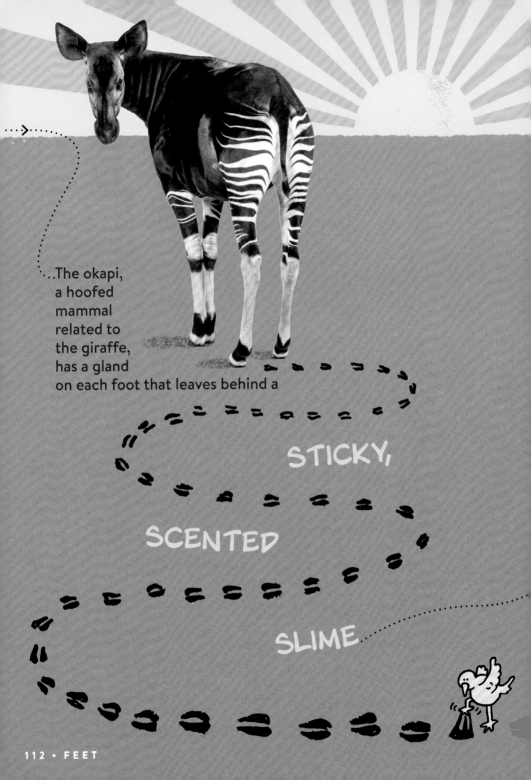

...The okapi, a hoofed mammal related to the giraffe, has a gland on each foot that leaves behind a

STICKY,

SCENTED

SLIME

Dogs have harmless bacteria on their feet that make them smell like

corn chips

BowWOW!

Dogs prefer to poop facing either **north or south**, which they can locate because they are sensitive to Earth's magnetic fields. Scientists aren't sure why dogs do this......

Mother dogs will **throw up food** they've eaten and allow their pups to eat the vomit.

Dogs learn the age, health, and mood of other dogs by **sniffing their rear ends**.

What's behind you?

To the toilet

Go to page 42

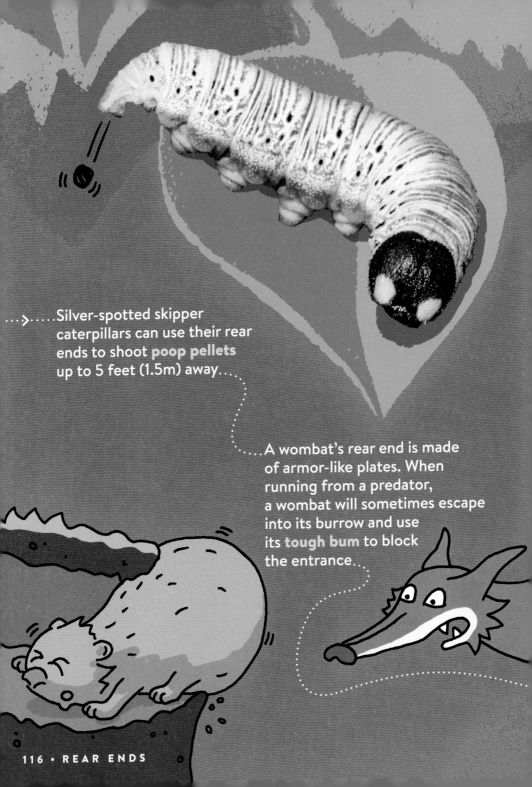

Silver-spotted skipper caterpillars can use their rear ends to shoot **poop pellets** up to 5 feet (1.5m) away...

A wombat's rear end is made of armor-like plates. When running from a predator, a wombat will sometimes escape into its burrow and use its **tough bum** to block the entrance.

There's a type of sea worm that has a pair of eyes on its rear end.

The Fitzroy River turtle can breathe through its butt

I see

Baby dragonflies move underwater by sucking water into their rear ends and then shooting it back out.

"Rheum" is the medical term for **eye boogers**

Achoo!

Giraffes can use their long tongues to *pick* their noses.

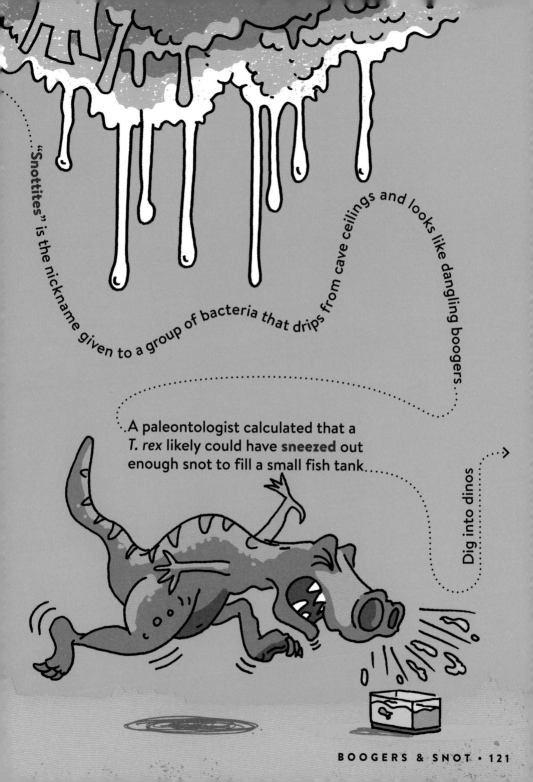

"Snottites" is the nickname given to a group of bacteria that drips from cave ceilings and looks like dangling boogers...

A paleontologist calculated that a *T. rex* likely could have **sneezed** out enough snot to fill a small fish tank...

Dig into dinos

Scientists have discovered fossilized **"blood worms"**—tiny parasites they believe lived in a dinosaur's blood and feasted on its bones....

The **dinosaur poop** in the movie *Jurassic Park III* was made from oatmeal.

.... Some dinosaurs had

FLEAS

that were 10 times as big as fleas today....

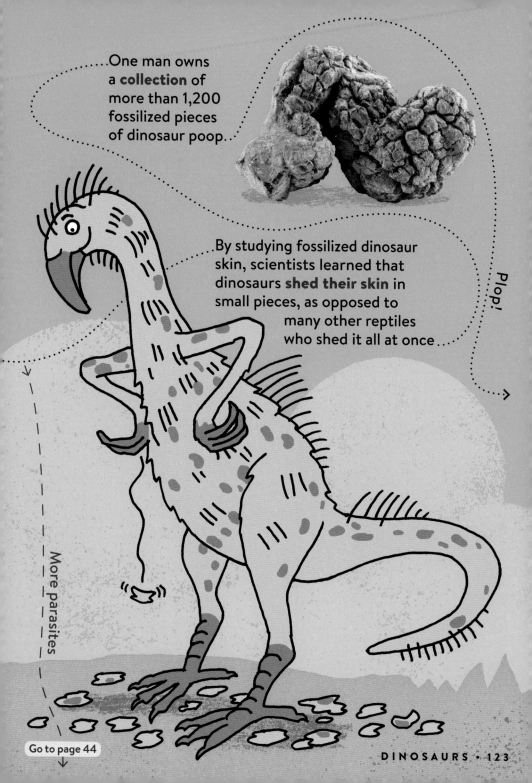

One man owns a **collection** of more than 1,200 fossilized pieces of dinosaur poop.

Plop!

By studying fossilized dinosaur skin, scientists learned that dinosaurs **shed their skin** in small pieces, as opposed to many other reptiles who shed it all at once.

More parasites

Go to page 44

A study found that at any given time, poop might account for up to 20 percent of the body weight of a **snake**.

On average, there are around the same number of **bacteria** in every human's **body** as there are cells.

A flashlight fish's **organs** have **bacteria** inside that make the animal's eyes glow blue.

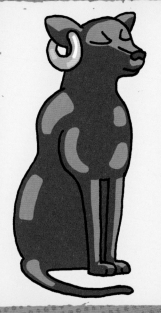

Archaeologists found the **body** of a mummified cat inside a cat-shaped statue that once wore a **gold** earring.

The chimera is a mythological monster with a live **snake** for a tail and a goat head growing out of its back, according to Greek **legend**.

Legend has it that Queen Cleopatra of ancient Egypt often bathed in donkey **milk**.

Russian folklore says that to keep **milk** fresh you should put a **frog** in the milk bucket.

Some species of **frog** can't vomit. Instead they eject their entire stomach and wipe off the **organ** while it hangs out of their mouth, before putting it back inside their body.

Stolen from a British palace, a solid **gold toilet** worth one million dollars was never recovered.

Exhibits on the history of **toilets** around the world are on display at the Sulabh International Museum of Toilets in New Delhi, India.

On display

The Mütter Museum in Philadelphia, Pennsylvania, features more than 1,300 "wet specimens," meaning preserved parts of the human body such as **hearts, brains, stomach organs,** and more.

Put your mind to it

Go to page 64

orld's longest **tapeworms** and a worm-infested dolphin stomach.

One museum in Missouri features wreaths, brooches, rings, bracelets, and art—all made of **human hair**.

Hairy situation

Located in Tasmania, Australia, the Pooseum features **poop collections** from many different animals.

Visitors to the Musée des Égouts in Paris, France can tour parts of the Parisian **sewer system**

Go to page 146

Scurry this way

...Archaeologists in Chile have found 800-year-old **combs** used to remove lice...

...French noblewomen in the 1700s wore **towering wigs** up to 2 feet (60cm) high and coated them in flour and grease that attracted fleas and lice... or sometimes even mice...

One ancient Egyptian recipe meant to **cure baldness** included cooking a worm in clay and then rubbing it on a person's head...

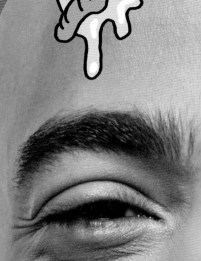

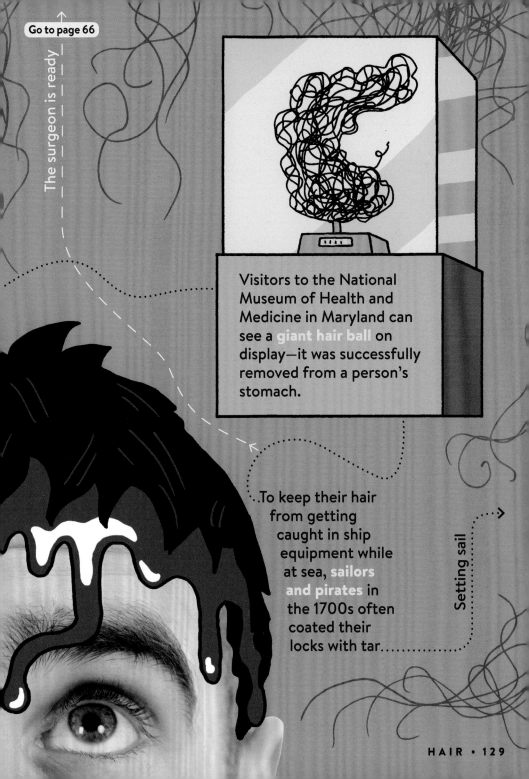

Go to page 66

The surgeon is ready

Visitors to the National Museum of Health and Medicine in Maryland can see a **giant hair ball** on display—it was successfully removed from a person's stomach.

To keep their hair from getting caught in ship equipment while at sea, **sailors and pirates** in the 1700s often coated their locks with tar.

Setting sail

For hundreds of years, Western sailors commonly **wiped their bottoms** with old pieces of rope called tow rags

.....The biscuits stored on board a ship, called hardtack, would often become so infested with maggots and weevils that they earned the nickname "**WORM CASTLES**"

It's an infestation!

One home in Georgia was once infested with more than **100,000 bees**—and 60 pounds (27kg) of honey! (The bees were safely removed and transported to another hive.)

Some houses have been infested by families of snakes who build their dens under the homes and slither through the walls.

There is a species of louse that only infests

CATS

Meow!

Hairless cats secrete so much oil from their skin that it can stain furniture.

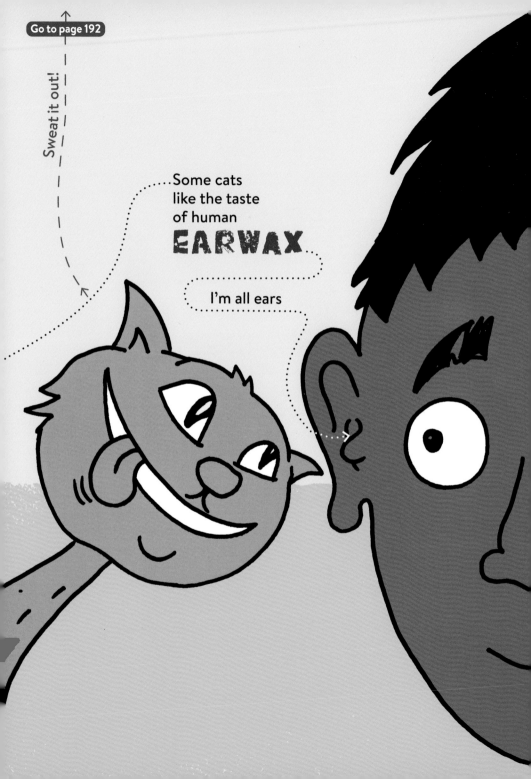

Go to page 192

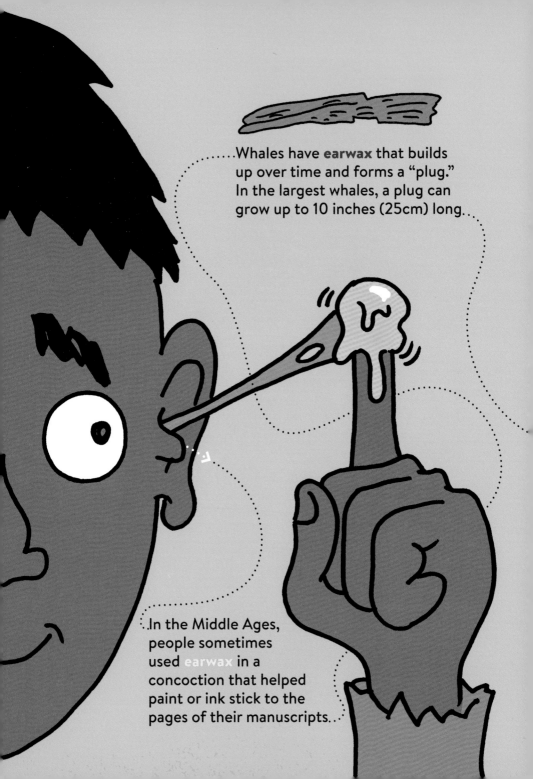

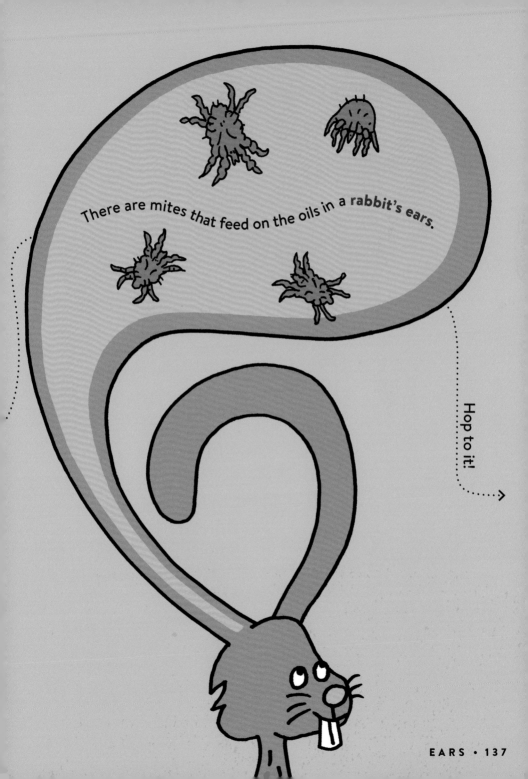

There are mites that feed on the oils in a rabbit's ears.

Hop to it!

Rabbits make **two types of poop:** a round, pellet-like poop, and a softer poop that they eat to get nutrition.

Paleontologists found vomit from a prehistoric whale that had been preserved for more than nine million years.

Scythian archers would sometimes dip the tips of their arrows in a mixture made with poop before battles.

Right whales have reddish orange poop.

The platypus doesn't have a stomach. Instead, mashed-up food travels directly from its mouth to its intestines without being broken down by acid.

There are glands that secrete venom on the hind legs of the male platypus.

A horse's stomach can become infested by hundreds of parasitic bot flies at a time.

Some flies kill their ant prey by cutting off their heads.

A famous philosopher's mummified body has been on display for nearly 200 years at a London school. But his head kept getting stolen as a prank, so the university locked it inside a safe.

During **battles**, medieval soldiers in castles would sometimes pour hot sand or boiling water on attackers in order to **defend** themselves.

Japanese honeybees can **defend** their hive from a **giant hornet** by surrounding it and using their body heat to cook the hornet to death.

An Asian **giant hornet** can grow to have a wingspan about half the size of an adult's **hand**.

Scientists are developing **cures** for multiple diseases using **venom** from snakes, jellyfish, and spiders.

In North America in the late 1800s and early 1900s, people with chapped **hands** and sores sometimes rubbed old sour cream on them as a **cure**.

Scientists at an American **university** have figured out how to turn bacteria and algae oil into a material that can be made into **shoes**.

Shoes have been used instead of plates to serve food at one restaurant in Las Vegas, Nevada.

Ready to order?

Go to page 136

You heard that right!

A hospital-themed restaurant in Latvia served food shaped like **body parts**—including tongues, eyeballs, and ears.

At a zombie-themed restaurant in Iowa, diners can order burgers with spooky names–previous specials featured gory-looking toppings like pasta with tomato sauce, baked beans, and **'zombie sauce'**.

Braaaaains

For fun, one chemist designed a recipe for a **perfume** intended to smell like rotting flesh. It's meant to hide the wearer from zombies.

The voodoo wasp lays its eggs inside the body of a caterpillar. When the larvae hatch, they **take over the caterpillar's mind** in order to force it to protect them, turning it into a zombie.

According to '80s popular culture, zombies eat brains to "**numb the pain**" of being undead...

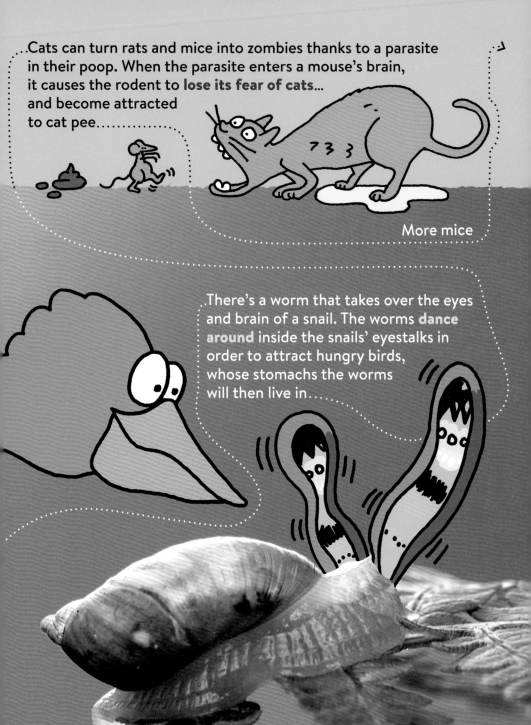

...Cats can turn rats and mice into zombies thanks to a parasite in their poop. When the parasite enters a mouse's brain, it causes the rodent to **lose its fear of cats...** and become attracted to cat pee..............

More mice

...There's a worm that takes over the eyes and brain of a snail. The worms **dance around** inside the snails' eyestalks in order to attract hungry birds, whose stomachs the worms will then live in...........

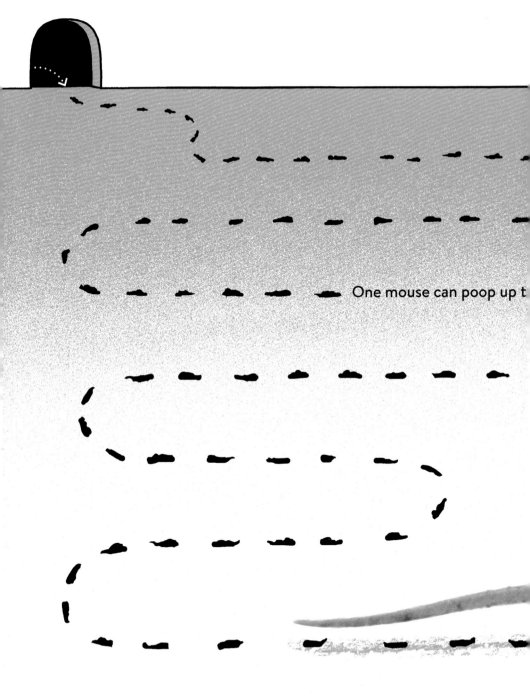

One mouse can poop up t

100 TIMES a day

Mice can't **burp** ⋯⋯ Excuse me!

Go to page 58

Blast off!

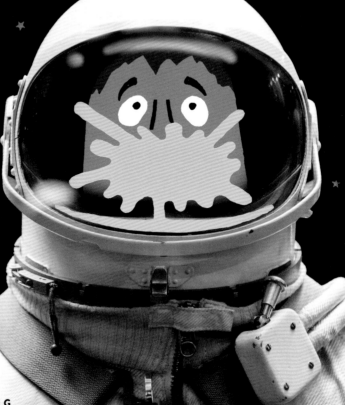

The **longest burp** ever recorded lasted just over 1 minute and 13 seconds....

If an astronaut burps in space, they produce what's known as a "**wet burp**": a mixture of air and whatever food or liquid they have in their stomach.

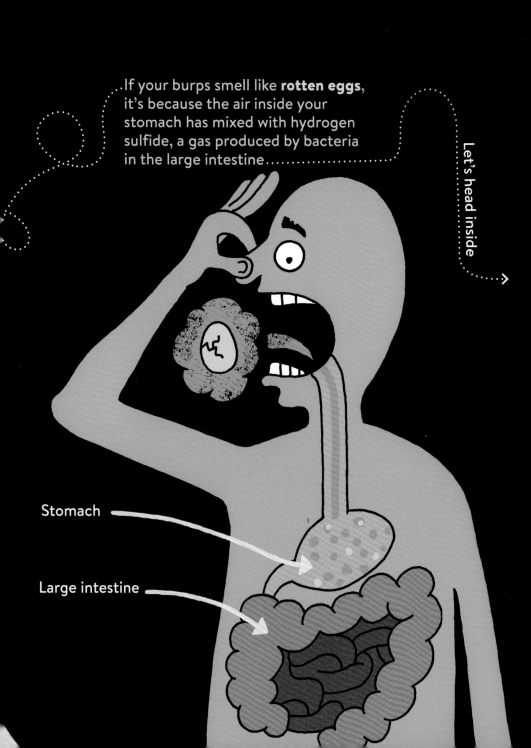

If your burps smell like **rotten eggs**, it's because the air inside your stomach has mixed with hydrogen sulfide, a gas produced by bacteria in the large intestine.

Let's head inside >

Stomach

Large intestine

Go to page 50

The **human liver** creates about enough bile—a fluid that helps digest food—to fill a one-quart (0.9L) milk carton every day.

Speaking of dairy

Your internal organs actually move around inside of you when you ride a **roller coaster**.

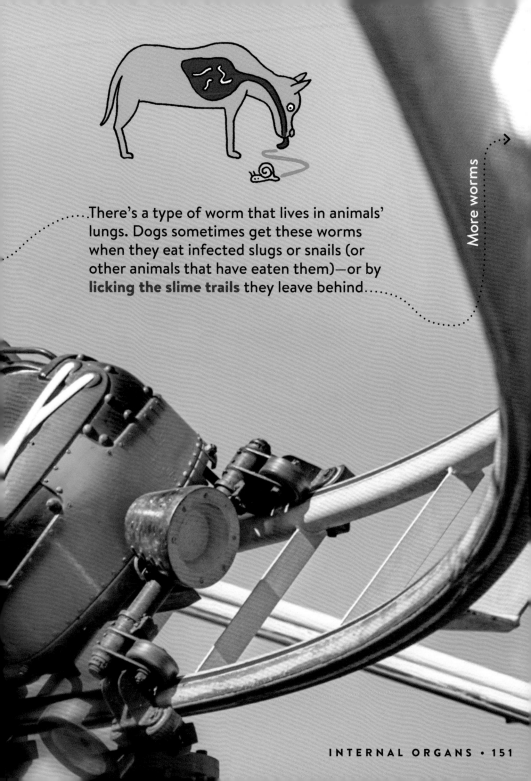

There's a type of worm that lives in animals' lungs. Dogs sometimes get these worms when they eat infected slugs or snails (or other animals that have eaten them)—or by **licking the slime trails** they leave behind.

More worms

One species of Australian earthworm is **bright blue**

Mud blister worms infest ocean mollusks such as oysters and clams by **burrowing into their shells** and creating a network of tunnels.

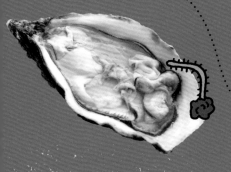

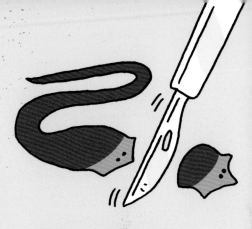

Planarian flatworms can **regrow their heads** if they are cut off... as well as an entirely new body from the severed head...

The tiny deep-sea worm *Chaetopterus pugaporcinus* is nicknamed the **"pigbutt worm"** because it looks like a pig's rear end...

Off to Australia

Found in Australia, the giant **Gippsland earthworm** can grow longer than most adults are tall...

More on behinds

Go to page 116

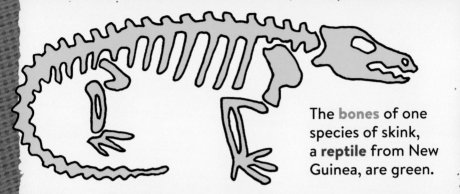

The **bones** of one species of skink, a **reptile** from New Guinea, are green.

Australia's Tasmanian devil will eat and digest every part of its prey— including the hair and **bones**.

The strongest known material in nature is found in the **teeth** of a type of marine **snail**.

Snakes are sometimes **eaten** by **scorpions**.

Some **snails** can survive being **eaten** by other animals.

Many **reptiles** are gastroliths, meaning they grind up their food with **rocks** they've swallowed.

A brown **rock** found by fossil hunters turned out to be part of a fossilized dinosaur **brain**.

Some **birds**, such as chickens, can be born with a genetic mutation that makes them grow **teeth**.

Praying mantises sometimes devour the **brains** of **birds**.

An ancient type of **scorpion** lived underwater and could grow larger than an adult human.

That's huge!

Some rhinoceroses **poop in shared piles**—calle

Between two and four million years ago, South Americ

In Oregon, there is an enormous **parasitic fungus** that stretches as wi

iddens—that can reach up to 65 feet (20m) across...

as home to a **"megarodent"**: a rodent the size of a bull...

Freaky fungi

78 American football fields. It's the largest living thing on Earth.......

Go to page 152

Real worms this way

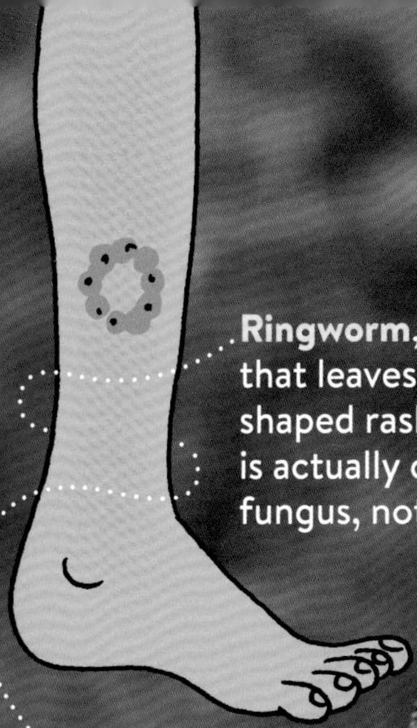

Ringworm, an infection that leaves an itchy, circle-shaped rash in humans, is actually caused by a fungus, not a worm.

A type of black, lumpy fungi that grow on rotting wood is known as **dead man's fingers.**

On to the undead

Go to page 144

...The
StARFISH FUNGUS
has "tentacles" covered in slime that emit a stinky smell to attract insects who spread the fungus's spores...

...The *Gyromitra esculenta* mushroom is incredibly poisonous and looks like a **human brain**...

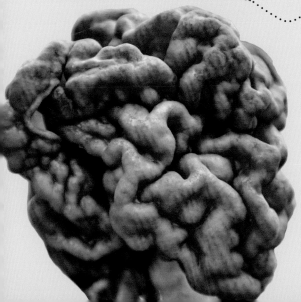

According to legend, there is a **mushroom-devouring creature** in the northeastern United States—called the Wapaloosie—that resembles a caterpillar mixed with a rodent...

Yikes!

In some Aboriginal mythologies of Australia, the Yara-ma-yha-who is a bloodsucking, vampire-like creature that is **part man and part frog or leech**.

According to folklore in South Africa, the impundulu is a bird that **sets its own fat on fire to cause lightning**.

Said to roam the marshes of Pennsylvania, U.S.A., the **mythical squonk** supposedly has webbed feet, a piglike nose, and loose-fitting skin covered in warts.

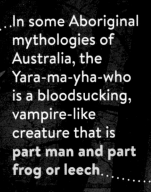

Freaky feet

Go to page 112

...The **hodag** of Wisconsin is said to have the face of a frog, the horns of a bull, and the back of a dinosaur—and to smell like a skunk and rotting meat...

In ancient Greek mythology, the gorgons were winged women who had

SNAKES FOR HAIR

Hisssss

Snakes are sometimes born with two heads.

...hich may attack or even try to eat each other.

Need a napkin? →

Snakes swallow their prey whole—and can **extend their jaws** to eat animals much larger than themselves, such as cows.

........>.......... **Hyenas** use their powerful jaws to smash and devour their prey's bones. In their stomachs, strong acid dissolves the bone shards...

...After eating, **Komodo dragons** often vomit up the horns, hooves, and other undigestible parts of their prey............

Feeling queasy

Go to page 48

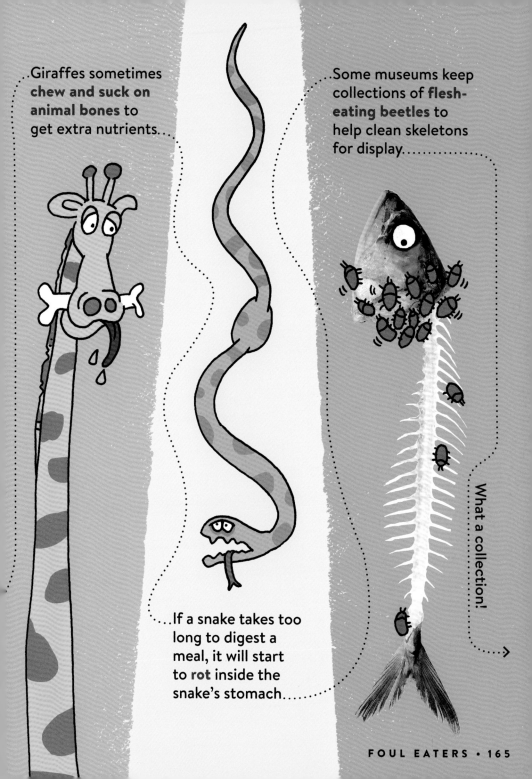

Giraffes sometimes **chew and suck on animal bones** to get extra nutrients...

Some museums keep collections of **flesh-eating beetles** to help clean skeletons for display...

What a collection!

...If a snake takes too long to digest a meal, it will start to **rot** inside the snake's stomach...

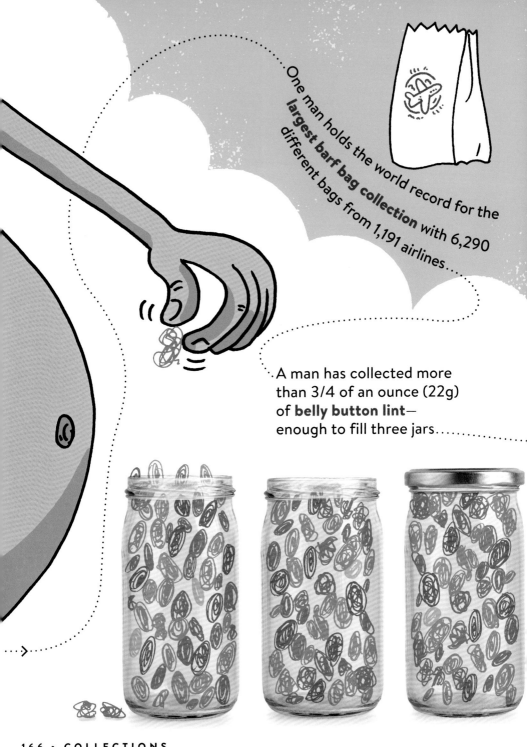

One man holds the world record for the **largest barf bag collection** with 6,290 different bags from 1,191 airlines...

A man has collected more than 3/4 of an ounce (22g) of **belly button lint**— enough to fill three jars...

Nailed it!

One man
collected his own

**NAIL
CLIPPINGS**

in a jar for more
than 35 years.

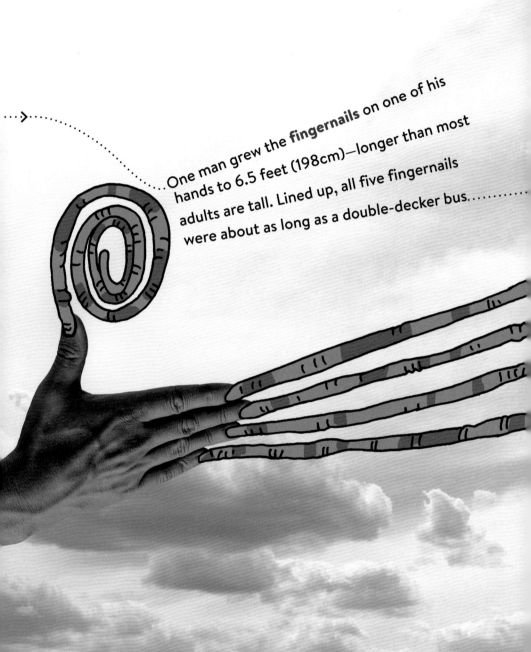

One man grew the **fingernails** on one of his hands to 6.5 feet (198cm)—longer than most adults are tall. Lined up, all five fingernails were about as long as a double-decker bus.

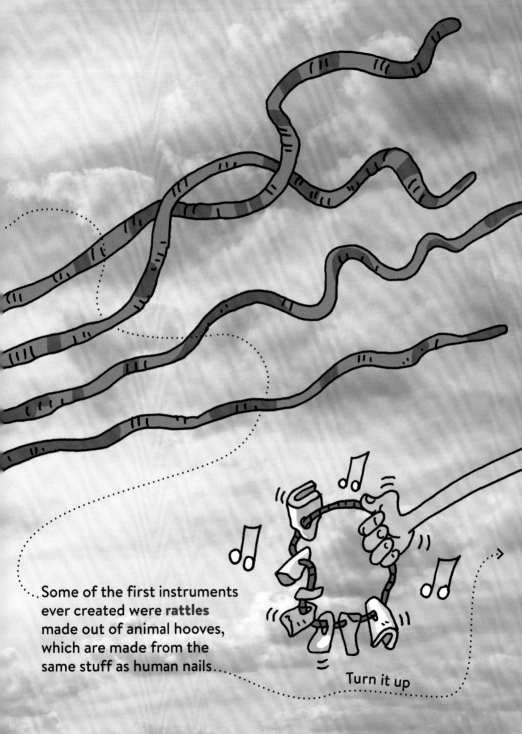

Some of the first instruments ever created were **rattles** made out of animal hooves, which are made from the same stuff as human nails.

Turn it up

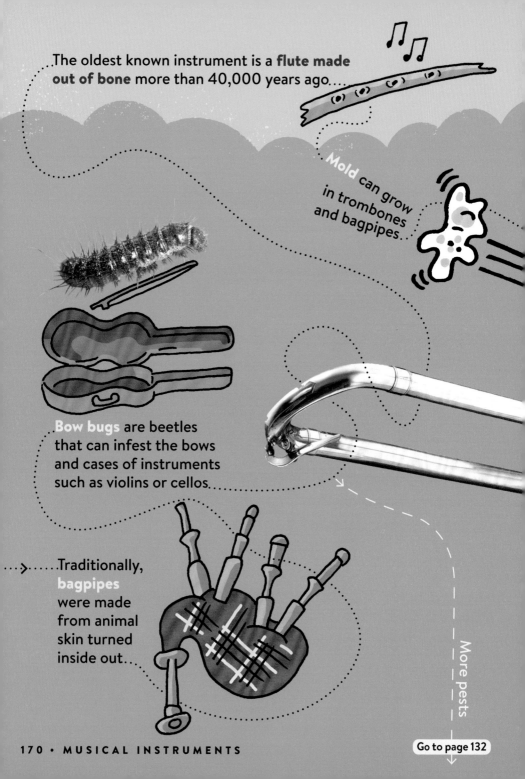

The oldest known instrument is a **flute made out of bone** more than 40,000 years ago.

Mold can grow in trombones and bagpipes.

Bow bugs are beetles that can infest the bows and cases of instruments such as violins or cellos.

Traditionally, **bagpipes** were made from animal skin turned inside out.

More pests

Go to page 132

Go to page 158

Follow the fungi →

The strings of musical instruments like violins used to be made from

sheep intestine

Baaaa →

Some **bird** parents remove their chicks' poop from their **home** by eating it.

Some architects are designing **homes** made from **trash**.

In New Zealand, sheep sometimes have their back fat fed upon— while they are still alive—by a type of **bird** called the kea.

An artificial **stomach** that actually digests food has been created by **scientists**.

Bees create honey by storing nectar in a special **stomach**, and then throwing it up into another bee's mouth. This repeats until one bee finally deposits it into the honeycomb!

Scientists found the remains of an entire snake in 1,500-year-old fossilized human **poop**—meaning it was likely eaten whole.

By studying fossilized **poop**, scientists learned that a dinosaur they previously thought was a vegetarian actually liked to eat **crustaceans**.

A type of **crustacean** related to sand fleas has a reflective coating that makes it practically **invisible**.

Scientists have created **trash**-eating **robots** that help clean rivers and beaches.

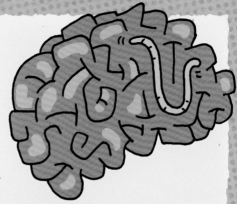

Scientists have developed a **robot** the size and shape of a thread that is designed to travel through the **blood** in a person's brain.

Bears attack hives not just for honey—they also eat the larvae and **bees**.

Up to 40,000 **moths** can be devoured in a single day by just one grizzly **bear**.

Mammal **blood** is the main meal of one type of **moth** that uses its sharp mouth to pierce the skin.

Gross on display

A Korean photographer lets **mold** grow on the pictures he takes, creating unique art.

There are **invisible** kinds of **mold**.

One famous artist created a series of paintings using **urine**

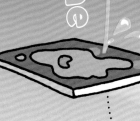

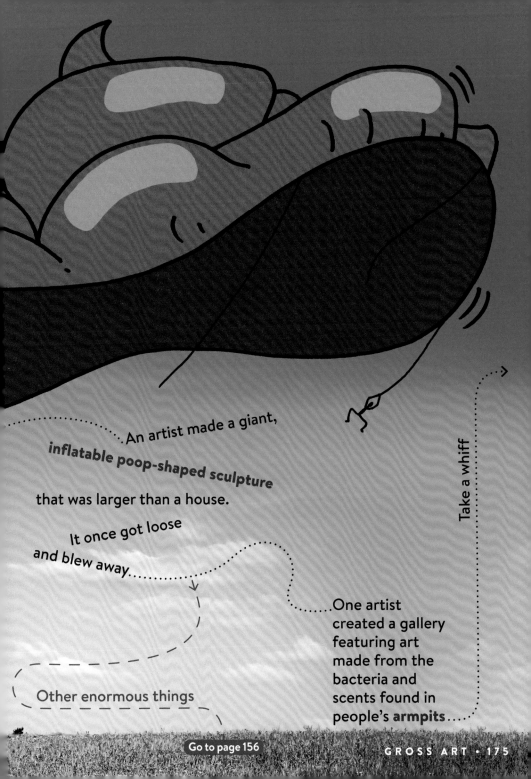

An artist made a giant, **inflatable poop-shaped sculpture** that was larger than a house.

It once got loose and blew away.

Other enormous things

Go to page 156

One artist created a gallery featuring art made from the bacteria and scents found in people's **armpits**.

Take a whiff

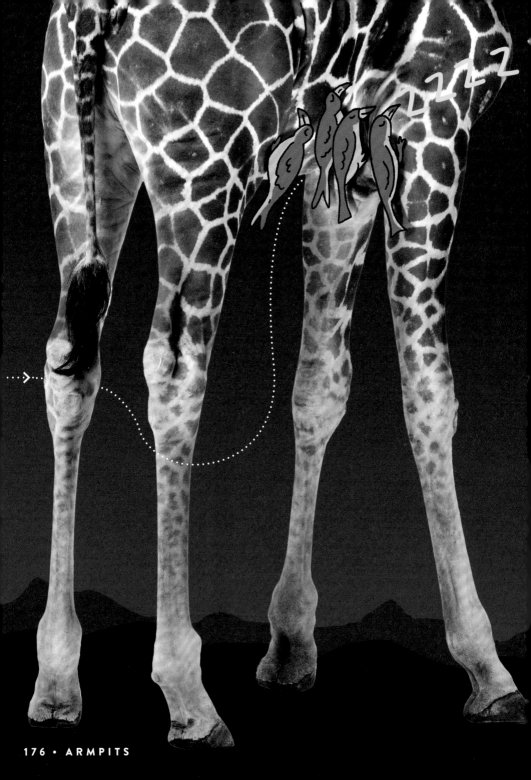

ZZZZZ Yellow-billed oxpeckers sometimes **sleep** in a giraffe's armpits.

How tweet

When the blue-capped ifrita feeds on poisonous insects and plants, it stores their toxins in its feathers and skin—**making itself poisonous** to any potential predators.

In Brazil, one type of parakeet lives in abandoned **termite nests** and snacks on the nutrient-rich dirt.

Some types of vultures keep cool by pooping on themselves

The shrike bird kills its prey by **spearing** it on sharp twigs.

Rub-a-dub

Birds often take

DUST BATHS

—they coat themselves in dirt to smother mites.

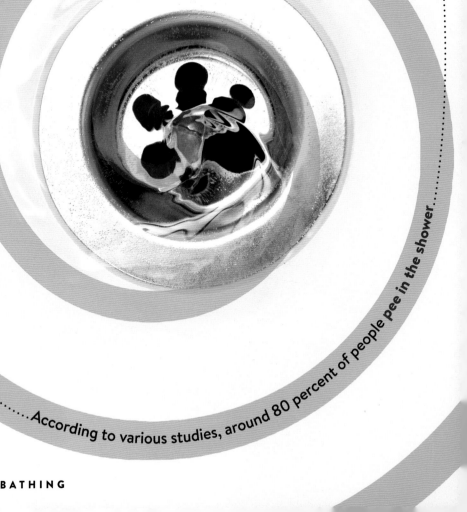

Go to page 90

When you gotta go

According to various studies, around 80 percent of people pee in the shower.

Many animals—
like pigs, hippos,
and elephants—
wallow in mud
to stay cool.

Play in the mud ······>

Students at some universities in the U.S.A play **OOZEBALL**, a version of volleyball played in muddy pits.

June 29 is **International Mud Day**.

Time to celebrate!

Go to page 198

Telling the future

A Celtic Halloween tradition involves cooking a stick, a coin, and a rag in a potato dish to **tell the fortunes** of the people who eat it.

Italy's Battle of the Oranges is a **three-day food fight** where people throw oranges at each other.

In Icelandic tradition, **Pot Licker** is a gift-giving, Christmastime prankster—known as a Yule Lad—who steals unwashed dishes and licks them clean.

April 23 is International Nose Picking Day.

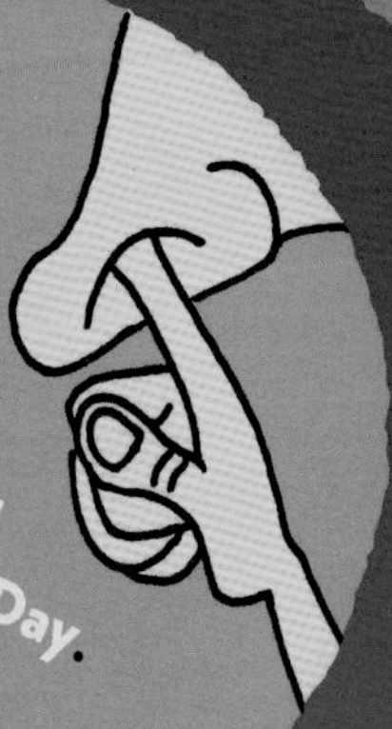

Feeling lucky? ⟩

In parts of Spain, figures of people pooping (including famous figures) are displayed at Christmastime for good luck (and for fun).

More snot
Go to page 120

In many parts of the world, it is considered good luck to be **pooped on by a bird**.

In the late 1800s in Britain and the U.S.A., it was considered good luck for a **bride** to have a hair from each member of her family sewn into her wedding dress....

Go to page 108

Dress to impress

For good luck, one American football player once wore the **same pair of gloves** for 11 games without washing them.

Game on

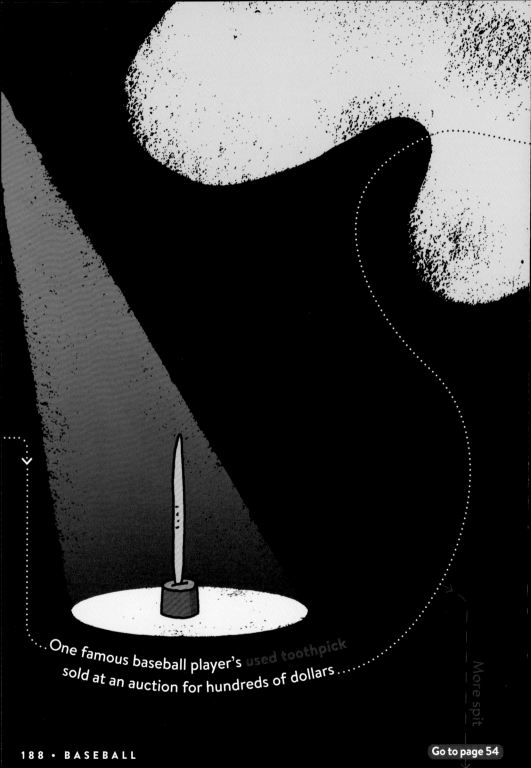

One famous baseball player's used toothpick sold at an auction for hundreds of dollars.....

More spit

Go to page 54

SOME BASEBALL PLAYERS PEE ON THEIR HANDS TO TOUGHEN THEM UP

Gotta go

Some farmers spray fox pee around their plants because the **smell** keeps hungry animals away.

The **smell** of stinky socks attracts a species of jumping **spider**.

The giant anteater's **tongue** reaches up to two feet (60cm) long, allowing it to scoop **ants** out of their nests.

A 2,000-year-old **mummy** uncovered in Egypt had a **tongue** made out of gold.

A colony of **ants** that had been trapped in an abandoned bunker survived by eating each other. The colony even grew to almost a **million** in number.

Artificial **spider** silk made out of bacteria has been created by **scientists**.

Scientists developed a type of glue for surgeries inspired by **slug** slime.

Scientists found **liquid** blood still inside the 42,000-year-old **mummy** of a horse.

A marine **slug** called a sea hare produces a toxic purple or red **liquid** to fend off enemies.

A collector once paid over $1.5 **million** for a sweat-stained costume from the *Wizard of Oz* movie.

Don't sweat it

Thanks to a special protein, horse sweat often lathers into a foam...

It's not just humans—**apes and monkeys** also sweat from their armpits.

Let's monkey around

Some monkeys have been seen using sticks to PICK THEIR NOSES

Feeling nosy?

...In order to develop **robots** with working "noses," scientists are trying to artificially reconstruct mucus...

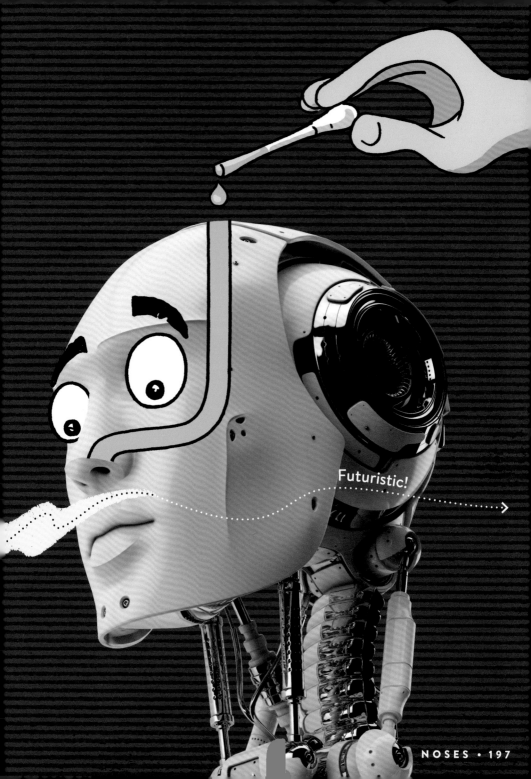

Futuristic!

Scientists are learning how to turn human poop into **edible bacteria**, which might one day help people survive long voyages to Mars.

Go to page 58

Out of this world

In the future,
you may be able to
3D-PRINT
your own meals from a
moldable paste.

One company wants to create a robot that brings you a fresh roll of **toilet paper** whenever you run out.

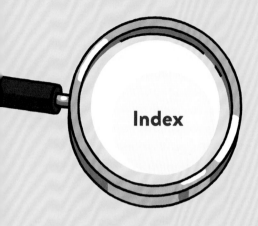

Index

Trademark notices
Jell-O is a trademark of The Kraft Heinz Company
Wizard of Oz is a trademark of Metro-Goldwyn-Meyer Studios Inc
Jurassic Park is a trademark of Universal City Studios LLC and Amblin Entertainment Inc
Tough Mudder is a trademark of Spartan Race Inc

Meet the FACTopians

Paige Towler is an author and editor based in Washington, D.C. A former editor for National Geographic Kids Books, she writes poetry about animals doing yoga, weird facts about the world, and silly stories about snakes and bats. When thinking about which foul facts to include in *Gross FACTopia!*, Paige took inspiration from all her favorite subjects: history, animals, strange science, monsters, and more. Her favorite fact in this book is that dung beetles sometimes "dance" on balls of poop.

Andy Smith is an award-winning illustrator. A graduate of the Royal College of Art, London, U.K., he creates artwork that has an optimistic, handmade feel. Andy loved drawing the slime, splats, and smells of *Gross FACTopia!* As an untidy person himself, he was most impressed with the frog that pops its stomach out of its mouth to give it a clean. His favorite fact to draw was the mud splattered oozeball game.

Lawrence Morton is an art director and designer based in London, U.K. He likes making words look fun and carefully created a trail of dots through the pages to help the reader navigate safely as they embark on their journey through this book. After reading about the behavior of baby sharks in their mothers' wombs, he needed to make himself a strong cup of tea.

Sources

Scientists and other experts are discovering new foul facts and updating icky information all the time. This is why our FACTopia team has checked that every fact in this book is based on multiple trustworthy sources and their work has been verified by a team of Britannica fact-checkers. Of the hundreds of sources used in this book, here is a list of key websites we consulted.

News Organizations
abcnews.go.com
australiangeographic.com.au
bbc.com
bbc.co.uk
businessinsider.com
cbsnews.com
cnn.com
discovermagazine.com
forbes.com
huffpost.com
iflscience.com
livescience.com
nationalgeographic.com
nationalgeographic.org
nbcnews.com
newscientist.com
npr.org
nytimes.com
pbs.org
phys.org
sciencealert.com
sciencedaily.com
sciencedirect.com
sciencemag.org
sciencing.com
scientificamerican.com
theatlantic.com
theguardian.com
vox.com
washingtonpost.com
wired.com

Government, Scientific, and Academic Organizations
acs.org
audubon.org
britannica.com
cdc.gov
gutenberg.org
journals.plos.org
jstor.org
mayoclinic.org
merriam-webster.com
nasa.gov
nature.com
ncbi.nlm.nih.gov
nih.gov
onlinelibrary.wiley.com
pubmed.ncbi.nlm.nih.gov
researchgate.net

Museums and Zoos
muttermuseum.org
nhm.ac.uk
ocean.si.edu
sandiegozoo.org
si.edu
smithsonianmag.com

Universities
academic.oup.com
berkeley.edu
mcgill.ca
stanford.edu
uchicago.edu
ucl.ac.uk
ufl.edu

Other Websites
atlasobscura.com
guinnessworldrecords.com
healthline.com
modernfarmer.com
natgeokids.com
ripleys.com
tripadvisor.com
webmd.com

Picture Credits

The publisher would like to thank the following for permission to reproduce their photographs and illustrations. While every effort has been made to credit images, the publisher apologizes for any errors or omissions and will be pleased to make any necessary corrections in future editions of the book.

BRITANNICA
BOOKS

Britannica Books is an imprint of What on Earth Publishing,
published in collaboration with Britannica, Inc.
Allington Castle, Maidstone, Kent ME16 0NB, United Kingdom
30 Ridge Road Unit B, Greenbelt, Maryland, 20770, United States

First published in the United States in 2022

Written by Paige Towler
Illustrated by Andy Smith
Designed by Lawrence Morton
Edited by WonderLab Group, LLC
Picture research by Annette Kiesow
Indexed by Connie Binder

Encyclopaedia Britannica
Alison Eldridge, Managing Editor; Michele Rita Metych,
Fact-Checking Supervisor; Will Gosner, Fact-Checker

Britannica Books
Nancy Feresten, Publisher; Natalie Bellos, Executive Editor; Meg Osborne, Assistant Editor;
Andy Forshaw, Art Director; Alenka Oblak, Production Manager

Library of Congress Cataloging-in-Publication Data available upon request

ISBN: 9781913750688

Printed in India

1 3 5 7 9 10 8 6 4 2

whatonearthbooks.com
britannica-books.com